DOS Made Easy

DOS Made Easy

Herbert Schildt

Osborne **McGraw-Hill**
Berkeley, California

Osborne **McGraw-Hill**
2600 Tenth Street
Berkeley, California 94710
U.S.A.

For information on translations and book distributors outside of the U.S.A.,
write to Osborne **McGraw-Hill** at the above address.

A complete list of trademarks appears on page 279.

DOS Made Easy

ISBN 0-07-881295-X

CONTENTS

PREFACE

This book is for anyone who wants to learn how to use DOS. It assumes no prior experience with computers. (More knowledgeable readers can skip the first two chapters.) DOS is a complex program with many commands and options. This book distills the most useful components of DOS and concentrates on getting you started with the program as quickly and easily as possible. By the time you finish this book, you will be using DOS like a pro.

There are many versions of DOS in use. This book covers all versions including 3.30, which is used on IBM's new PS/2 line of computers. No matter what computer you have, if it runs DOS, you can use this book.

You will begin with the basics, including complete discussions of what DOS is and what it does. Then, you will learn the essential DOS commands. Understanding these few commands enables you to begin using the computer. As you continue, you will learn to use the DOS editor and will see how to create custom commands of your own. As you progress, you'll learn the more advanced DOS commands that give you real power over the system. The later chapters explain how to configure your system and how to manage your floppy and fixed drives — including backing up the fixed disk.

This book is tutorial in nature, with many hands-on examples and experiments. It is highly recommended that you have a computer available so that you can work along with the text. Although the examples are applicable to all versions of DOS, they reflect the IBM version of DOS, called PC-DOS, because it is the one with the largest user base. Because the fixed disk is so common, special emphasis has been placed on its use.

However, if you don't have a fixed disk, don't worry. All examples are explained for users with or without fixed disks.

The appendix contains a quick reference to the DOS commands. It will be a lasting resource as you become increasingly proficient with DOS.

—HS

COMPUTER BASICS

Before beginning your exploration of DOS, it is important to understand a few things about your computer, including the individual pieces of the computer and how they work together to form the complete system. Although you don't need to understand how a computer works to use it, it does help to have some familiarity with its basic operation. In this chapter, an IBM-style computer will be used for illustration, but the information is applicable to virtually all IBM-compatible computers.

The first three chapters of this book are intended for those readers who have no prior experience with computers or DOS. If you already know the basic components of your computer system and how to start DOS and understand the basic concepts of files and directories, you may want to skip to Chapter 4.

THE PARTS OF YOUR SYSTEM

All microcomputers consist of at least the following three items:

- The system unit
- The keyboard
- The monitor (video display screen)

These represent the minimal amount of equipment needed to create a functional computer. They are illustrated in Figure 1-1. In addition to these, most computer installations include a printer. Many computer systems also have a modem, which is used to allow two computers to communicate over a telephone line. Your computer could contain other devices, such as a mouse (used for pointing), a plotter, or a light pen.

THE SYSTEM UNIT

The system unit is the heart of the computer and is composed of the following items:

- The central processing unit (CPU)
- Memory
- Disk drives
- Various adapters and options

All other pieces of the computer plug into the system unit through connectors on the back. (If your computer is not set up and ready to run, refer to the installation guide provided with your system.)

The CPU

The central processing unit, or *CPU*, is the brain of the computer. It performs all the analytical, computational, and logical functions that occur inside the system. It operates by executing a program, which is a list of instructions. (We'll talk more about programs shortly.)

Memory

The memory of the computer stores information that will be processed by the CPU. The memory of your computer is made up of *bytes*. Although the origin of the term *byte* is lost in the past, it essentially means one character. Therefore, if someone says to you that your computer has

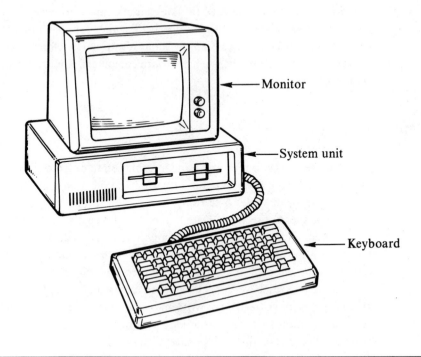

FIGURE 1-1   The basic elements of a computer

about 640,000 bytes of memory, it means that it can store approximately 640,000 characters.

You will often hear two terms associated with the memory of the computer: RAM and ROM. *RAM* stands for random access memory. This is the kind of memory your computer has the most of, and it may be used to store and retrieve any type of information. The one fact you should remember about RAM is that anything stored in it is lost when the computer is turned off.

The other type of memory contained in your computer is called *ROM,* which stands for read only memory. The contents of this sort of memory cannot be changed; they can only be read. ROM stores information that the computer needs when it is first turned on. (In a way, ROM in the computer is similar to instinct in an animal.) Unlike RAM, the contents of ROM are not lost when the computer is turned off.

Often you will see the letter *K* after a number when the amount of RAM in a computer is referred to. For example, most computers today come with 640K bytes of RAM. Loosely, K stands for 1000 and is the symbol used in the metric system to stand for *kilo*. Therefore, 640K is short for 640,000. (Actually, when used with computers, K more precisely stands for 1024.)

Disk Drives

A disk drive is used to read and write information to or from a diskette. (The diskette actually holds the information and the drive is the mechanism that reads or writes data to or from it. You will learn more about diskettes in the next section.) Data that is stored on a diskette is not lost when the computer is turned off. Since anything that is in the RAM of the computer is lost when the power is turned off, information that is important and that you wish to keep must be stored on a diskette.

All disk drives have two elements in common. First, they use a *read/write head* to read and write information to the diskette. This read/write head is similar to the play/record head on a cassette tape recorder. Second, all disk drives have a means of spinning the diskette. Because information is spread over the surface of the diskette, the diskette must turn in order to access all the information on it.

There are two basic types of disk drives: floppy and fixed. They are housed in the system unit. Most system units are configured one of these four ways:

- One floppy disk drive
- Two floppy disk drives
- One floppy and one fixed disk drive
- Two floppy disk drives and one fixed disk drive

These configurations are illustrated in Figure 1-2.

Before the advent of the IBM Personal System/2 Model 60 and Model 80, the system unit of most personal computers sat on the desk beneath the monitor. With the Model 60 and Model 80, however, the system unit is usually placed on the floor away from the monitor and keyboard. The disk drives are mounted sideways in the system unit. These

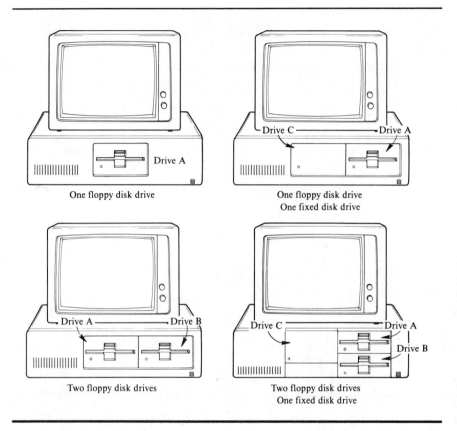

FIGURE 1-2   Disk drive configurations

models may also come with an external 5 1/4-inch drive to allow the easy exchange of information with older IBM PC and AT computers.

The drives in a system are labeled by letters, as also shown in Figure 1-2. Generally, the fixed disk drive is drive C.

The floppy disk drives use *diskettes* as their storage media. A diskette is a thin, flat, removable magnetic disk that stores information. There are two types of floppy diskettes. The older, but currently the most common, is the 5 1/4-inch minifloppy. This is the type used by the IBM PC, XT, and AT and compatibles. A new type of floppy disk is the 3 1/2-inch microfloppy, which is used by IBM's newer System/2 line of computers. Diskette elements are shown in Figure 1-3.

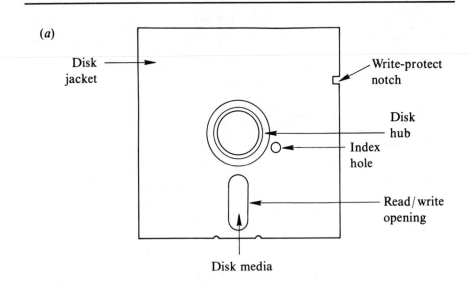

(a)

Disk jacket

Write-protect notch

Disk hub

Index hole

Read/write opening

Disk media

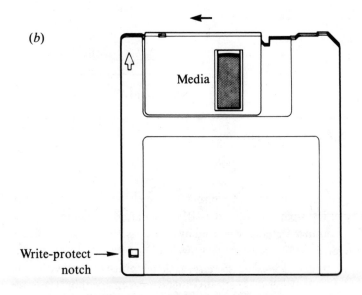

(b)

Media

Write-protect notch

FIGURE 1-3   Elements of (a) 5 1/4-inch minifloppy and (b) 3 1/2-inch micro-floppy diskettes

Minifloppy Diskettes

The 5 1/4-inch minifloppy diskette, as shown in Figure 1-3, consists of a magnetic medium that actually stores the information, surrounded by a stiff jacket that protects the magnetic medium from harm. The computer accesses the magnetic medium through the *read/write opening*. The *index hole* is used by the computer to properly align the diskette. Perhaps the single most important feature of the diskette is the *write-protect notch*. When the write-protect notch is left uncovered (as shown in the drawing), information can be both written to and read from the diskette. However, when this notch is covered using a *write-protect tab* (supplied along with the diskette), the computer can only read the information on the diskette, not write to the diskette. Covering the write-protect notch is a good way to prevent important information from being accidentally destroyed. Later in this book you will be instructed to cover the notch for this very reason.

You insert a minifloppy diskette into a disk drive with the write-protect notch to the left and the read/write hole facing forward. Before the computer can use the diskette, the drive door must be closed or *latched*. There are two basic types of 5 1/4-inch minidrives in general use; the method of closing the drive door for both is shown in Figure 1-4.

The diskette must be turning in order for the disk drive to read or write information from or to it. When you close the drive door, you are doing three things. First, you are telling the computer that there is a diskette in the drive. Second, you are securing the diskette to the turntable that actually spins the diskette. Finally, you are enabling the read/write head of the drive to access the diskette.

Microfloppy Diskettes

The IBM System/2 line of computers uses microfloppy diskettes. In principle, these work the same way that minifloppy diskettes do except that they are smaller and provide more protection for the magnetic medium. As Figure 1-3 shows, a microfloppy diskette has a *shutter* that covers the read/write opening. This shutter is opened by the computer only when access to the diskette is required. This protects the magnetic

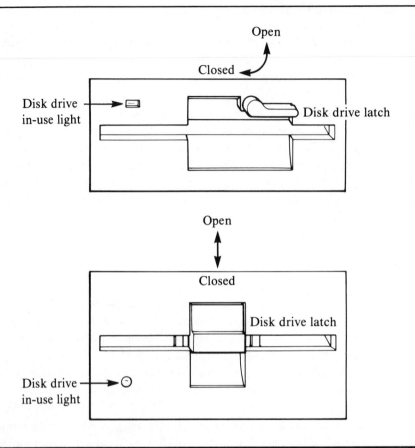

FIGURE 1-4   Closing the drive door

medium from harm while the diskette is outside the computer and from dust while it is inside the computer.

The write-protect notch in a microfloppy diskette has a built-in slider that is used to cover the notch. The write-protect notch in a microfloppy diskette works opposite to the way it does in a minifloppy diskette. When the notch is open, the diskette is write protected; otherwise it is not.

Handling Diskettes

No matter what type of diskette you have, you must take care to protect it from harm. The basic rules are no dust, no magnets, and no folding (see Figure 1-5). Motors in devices such as vacuum cleaners and floor waxers set up strong magnetic fields which can, given the right circumstances and proximity, erase a diskette. Never store your diskettes in the bottom drawer of your desk where they stand the greatest chance of being affected by these appliances.

Fixed Disks

Many computers contain a special type of disk drive called a *fixed disk*. You will also see this referred to as a *hard disk*. A fixed disk is a high-speed, large-capacity disk drive. The disk cannot be removed from the disk drive; hence the term *fixed*.

A fixed disk can hold substantially more information than a minifloppy or microfloppy diskette. For example, minifloppy or microfloppy diskettes typically hold between 360,000 and 1,440,000 bytes of information, whereas fixed disks hold between 10,000,000 and 70,000,000 bytes. In computerese, one million is referred to by the prefix *mega;* hence, you will often hear the amount of storage available on a fixed disk referred to in terms of *megabytes*. For example, a disk drive that can hold 20,000,000 bytes of information will be called a 20-megabyte drive.

An important fact to remember about fixed disks is that they do not like jolting vibrations or sharp shocks. A hard blow to the computer while it is accessing a fixed disk can damage the magnetic medium. The reason for this is that the read/write head of a fixed disk is positioned extremely close to the surface of the magnetic medium. If you jar it sharply, the head could actually come into contact with the medium and cause a scratch,

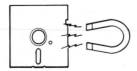

Never place diskettes near magnetic devices.

Always place diskettes back into a disk envelope when you are not using them.

Keep diskettes away from your telephone.

Store your diskettes in a safe location.

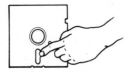

Never touch your floppy disk media.

Always make backup copies of your floppy disks.

Never smoke near floppy disks.

Keep room temperature in the range 50° F to 110° F.

Never bend floppy disks.

FIGURE 1-5   Protecting your diskettes

which could cause a loss of information. You don't have to walk around on tiptoes when using a fixed disk, but you should treat a fixed disk as what it is: a highly sophisticated piece of equipment.

THE MONITOR

The monitor is the television-like screen that generally sits on top of the system unit (except in the new IBM Model 60 and Model 80, where the system unit is usually placed on the floor instead of on the desk with the monitor and keyboard). As you can probably guess, the computer uses the monitor to display information — in other words, it is your window into the computer. The monitor plugs into the back of the system unit. There are two basic types of monitors: black-and-white monitors and color monitors. For the purposes of this book, it doesn't matter what type you have.

THE KEYBOARD

The keyboard allows you to communicate with the computer. There are two basic styles of keyboard commonly found with microcomputers: PC/XT-style keyboards and AT-style keyboards. The PC/XT-style keyboard was the first one developed by IBM. Later, the IBM AT computer was developed with a slightly different keyboard. Both types are shown in Figure 1-6. (The Personal System/2 keyboards are similar to the AT keyboard.) For the most part, these keyboards are like that of a typewriter. However, there are a few special features that you should be aware of.

The 10 keys on the far left of the PC/XT-style keyboard or the twelve keys on the top row of the AT-style keyboard, labeled F1 through F10 or F1 through F12, are called *function keys*. These, as well as other special keys, are gray instead of white like the rest of the keys. These keys have special meanings that depend upon what the computer is doing. The ESC, or *escape*, key can be used to cancel certain operations. The CTRL, or *control*, and ALT, or *alternate*, keys are used to generate special characters not readily available at the keyboard. The CAPS LOCK key operates the same way as it does on a typewriter by forcing all characters to be uppercase.

(a)

(b)

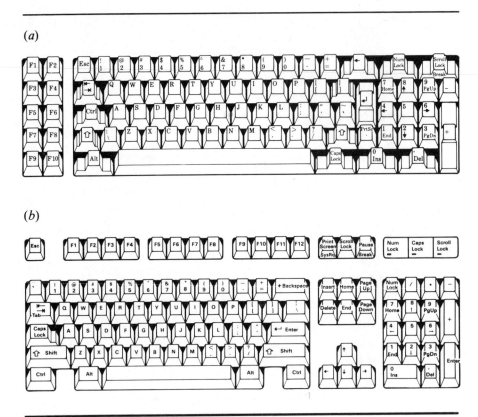

FIGURE 1-6   The two most common keyboard styles: (a) the PC/XT style and
(b) the AT style

The numeric keypad has two separate purposes. The first is to allow
the rapid entry of numbers; the other is to control the movements of the
cursor on the screen. Although the arrow keys are not fully used by DOS,
programs using DOS will use them. The NUM LOCK key determines
whether the arrow keys or the digit keys are active. By pressing the NUM
LOCK key, you can toggle between the two uses of the number pad.

The PRTSCR key causes what is currently on the computer screen to be
printed on the printer. The SCROLL LOCK-BREAK key is used to cancel
certain computer operations.

You will learn more about these special keys later, as you learn more
about DOS.

THE PRINTER

Most computer installations include a printer. As you might expect, the printer is used to create permanent output from the computer. It is possible that your computer will have more than one printer connected to it because different printers are used for different purposes. The most common printer is called a *dot matrix* printer. This sort of printer creates printouts quickly, but its print quality is not as good as that of a typewriter. Another type of printer is called either a *daisy wheel* or *letter-quality* printer. It creates high-quality output and is generally used in word processing applications. Finally, you might have a *laser* printer attached to your computer. A laser printer is capable of producing typeset-quality output and is used when only the very best output quality will do. No matter what type of printer you have, if it is connected to the computer in the standard way, everything you learn in this book will be applicable to it.

MISCELLANEOUS ATTACHMENTS

Many computer installations include devices and attachments other than the printer. You won't need any of these to fully utilize DOS or to use this book. However, the most common are the modem and the mouse, and we will take a brief look at them now.

The Modem

For a computer to communicate with another computer over the telephone lines, a piece of hardware called a *modem* is needed. There are two types of modem: internal and external. An internal modem is a special circuit card that plugs into the inside of the computer. All you will see is a telephone cord plugged into the back of the system unit. An external modem sits outside the system. DOS cannot directly communicate with a modem. If a modem is part of your computer, you will need a special communication program to run it.

The Mouse

A *mouse* is an alternate input device. Unlike the keyboard where you type
in information, the mouse is used to select various options. A mouse
consists of a small, hand-held unit with one, two, or three buttons and a
small ball on the bottom. As you move the mouse across your desk, a
small locator symbol (often cross hairs) moves across the screen. A
typical mouse is shown in Figure 1-7.

As with a modem, DOS cannot directly use a mouse, but other
programs operating under DOS can.

SOFTWARE

So far, we have discussed only the different pieces of hardware that make
up a computer system. However, there is a saying in the computer
business that "a computer without software is, at best, an expensive
doorstop." Software consists of programs, and programs run your com-

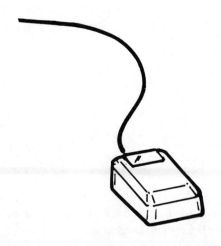

FIGURE 1-7   A typical mouse

puter. Without programs, the computer hardware can do nothing because it doesn't know what to do. The computer hardware can do nothing that it isn't told to do; it is the software's job to make the computer do useful things. You will probably use several programs, including word processors, accounting packages, and spreadsheets.

You do not need to know how to program to fully utilize DOS, but it is useful to understand what a program is and how a computer executes programs. A program consists of a sequence of instructions that the computer follows. When a program is run, all of its instructions are loaded into the memory of the computer. To begin execution, the CPU fetches the first instruction and does what it is told to do. Next, it gets the second instruction, performs that task, then it gets the third instruction, and so on. The program ends when the last instruction is executed.

Computer programs are represented in *machine code* that the computer can directly read and execute. Aside from very experienced and knowledgeable programmers, people cannot read and understand machine code. For this reason, most programs are written in what is called a *high-level language,* which is quite English-like. This high-level version of the program is translated into machine code by a special program called a *compiler.*

WHAT IS DOS AND WHAT DOES IT DO?

First and foremost, DOS is a program; it is part of the software that your computer needs to function. But it is a very special program because it is the program that is in charge of the computer's hardware. With very few exceptions, any other program that runs on your computer does so with the help of DOS. Stated a different way, DOS is the program that controls the basic hardware components of the computer.

Although DOS controls other programs that run in the computer, DOS is under your control and exists primarily to give you a way to communicate your instructions to the computer. You give instructions to DOS via commands that it will recognize. For the most part, these commands consist of regular, English-like words. For example, here are a few actual DOS commands: ERASE, COPY, and PRINT. In the next chapter you will learn several of the most important DOS commands.

DOS Versions

Like most things, DOS has changed over time. Since its creation, it has been improved and enhanced. Each time DOS was revised, a new version number was assigned to it. The first version of DOS was 1.00. The latest DOS version is 3.30, which was introduced with IBM's Personal System/2 line. If you have a PC, XT, AT, or compatible, you are probably using an earlier version. This book covers all versions of DOS from 1.00 through 3.30.

In versions of software the number preceding the decimal point is called the *major revision number.* This number is changed only when major alterations take place. The numbers to the right of the decimal point are called the *minor revision numbers,* and they indicate versions that differ only slightly from the previous one.

SUMMARY

You should now be familiar with

- The various pieces of a computer system
- The concept of programs and software
- The function DOS serves in the computer
- The way DOS version numbers are designed

In the next chapter you will learn to start the computer and to make backup copies of the DOS diskette as well as a few simple commands.

RUNNING DOS

In this chapter you will learn how to start DOS running on your computer. You will also learn two useful DOS commands. For this and the remaining chapters in this book, it will be best if you are seated at your computer so that you can try the examples.

ENTERING INFORMATION AND USING THE BACKSPACE KEY

Before beginning, it is important to understand how to enter information into the computer. As you will shortly see, there are many times when DOS will ask you a question. To answer the question you type your response at the keyboard. But DOS does not have any idea of what you are typing until you *enter it* by striking the ENTER key. In other words, until you press ENTER, DOS does not know what you have typed.

There is a very important advantage to this approach to entering information into DOS: It allows you to correct mistakes. DOS requires the information and commands you give it to be in a precise format; it does not accept misspellings, for instance. If you see that you have made a typing error—or if you change your mind about the command you want

17

to enter—you can correct it by using the BACKSPACE key, which is the gray key with the arrow pointing to the left (labeled BK on some keyboards), so long as you have not yet pressed ENTER. Each time you press BACKSPACE, the cursor backs up one space, erasing whatever was in that space. Once you have erased your error, you simply begin typing again.

So far as DOS is concerned, uppercase and lowercase letters are the same; that is, any time you communicate with DOS, you can enter information without worrying about what case the letters are. However, keep in mind that many programs that run under DOS are case sensitive and require entries to use either uppercase or lowercase characters.

LOADING DOS

To load DOS, first turn on the computer. If your computer has a fixed disk, DOS will automatically load from that disk; you don't have to do anything. Hence, there is no need to insert a diskette into drive A. The method for loading DOS from a floppy disk differs depending on the system and the version of DOS you are using.

Loading DOS 3.20 and Earlier

Many versions of DOS are supplied on two diskettes. For versions of DOS prior to 3.30, the disk you should put in the computer is simply labeled "DOS"; the other disk is labeled "Supplemental Programs" and is not required to run DOS. After you have turned on the computer, put the DOS diskette into drive A and close the door. The computer will then load DOS into memory and begin execution.

Loading Version 3.30

Version 3.30 is supplied on one 3 1/2-inch microfloppy for System/2 computers and on two 5 1/4-inch diskettes for PC, XT, AT, and compatible computers. To load DOS using a System/2 computer, turn on the computer and place the DOS diskette into drive A. (The 3 1/2-inch diskette is labeled "DOS" on the left and "Startup/Operating" on the right.) In the 5 1/4-inch diskette 3.30 version, DOS is split between two diskettes and both are required. (Version 3.30 is so large that it no longer fits on one 5 1/4-inch diskette.) To load DOS from two 5 1/4-inch disks, first place the disk labeled "Startup" into drive A. Once DOS has loaded and started execution, remove the Startup diskette and insert the diskette called "Operating" into the computer.

For ease of discussion, this book will use the phrase "DOS diskette" whether referring to a single diskette or to the two supplied with version 3.30 in the 5 1/4-inch version.

A word of warning: Precisely what happens next is determined by whether DOS is loaded from a fixed disk or from a DOS diskette. This is because DOS can be customized to better fit the needs of a specific working environment. (You will learn how to customize DOS later in this book.) If the computer you are using has been in use for a while and is used by other people, very likely some customization has occurred. No customization will affect the way you control DOS or use it to help you run programs, but it can cause some things to appear differently on the monitor or not to appear at all. As you read this chapter, if you find that your screen looks nothing like what is being shown in the book, you have two choices. First, you can place the original DOS diskette in drive A and so force the computer to load DOS from that diskette. Your screen will then show the examples as they appear in this chapter. Second, you can just ignore the differences and generalize what is presented here to what you see on your screen. Either way, after this chapter, there won't be any significant discrepancies. For the rest of this chapter, let's assume that you have loaded DOS from the DOS diskette.

As DOS begins execution, the screen will clear, and you will see the following printed on the screen (of course, the current date will be different):

```
Current date is Fri 5-08-1987
Enter new date (mm-dd-yy): _
```

The cursor will be positioned after the colon. The *cursor*, a small, blinking character that indicates where the next character will be printed on the screen, is represented here with the underscore character. For the remainder of this book, the underscore will be used to indicate the cursor's position. (The cursor may be represented as a block in certain computers, but the concept is the same.)

When DOS starts execution, it tells you what it thinks is the current date and prompts you for a new date in case the date it presents is incorrect. If the current data is the correct date, then you can simply press the ENTER key. Otherwise, you should enter the correct date in the common month-day-year format, using numbers for each part. For example, to enter the date February 28, 1989, you would type

```
2-28-89
```

You can also enter the date using slashes or periods to separate the parts. For example, you can enter 2/28/89. For reasons that will become clear, it is important that DOS know the correct date. Remember, if you make a typing error, use the BACKSPACE key to correct it.

If you accidentally enter a form that DOS cannot understand or an out-of-range date, DOS will print the message

```
Invalid date
```

and then prompt you again for the correct date.

Some computers are also equipped with a clock and calendar option. When present in the system, the clock and calendar option keep the correct time and date even when the computer is turned off. It is possible to make DOS check this option when it begins execution. If you do so, DOS will probably have the proper date. However, in systems without this option, DOS will always have the wrong date because it has no way of knowing what time it is when the computer is turned off. In this case, the date DOS presents to you will be the date that DOS was created.

After you have entered the date, you will see the following message:

```
Current time is 08:10:11.00
Enter new time: _
```

The time shown is the time that DOS thinks it is. (Remember, the time your system shows will be different.) The time is shown in the format

hours:minutes:seconds.hundredths of seconds

DOS uses a 24-hour clock. This means, for example, that 9 A.M. will be displayed as 9, but 1 P.M. will be displayed as 13, 2 P.M. as 14, and so on. The morning hours are displayed as on the common 12-hour clock, and the afternoon hours all have 12 added to them. If your system includes the clock and calendar option, the time will be correct. Otherwise, it will be wrong, and you will have to set it. When you set the clock, you enter only the hour, minutes, and seconds—you do not enter the hundredths of seconds. For example, if the actual time is 2:30 in the afternoon, you enter

`14:30:00`

After you have correctly entered the time, the DOS sign-on message will be displayed, and your screen will look like that shown in Figure 2-1. The screen shown is as it appears for DOS on the IBM PC family of computers. Your sign-on message may be slightly different.

THE SIGN-ON MESSAGE AND THE DOS PROMPT

The sign-on message tells you the version number of the DOS program you are using. Some DOS commands work only with later versions of DOS, so it is a good idea to know what version you are running. You should make a mental note of it at this time.

Beneath the sign-on message and on the far left, you will see either A> or C>. If you loaded DOS from a diskette, then you will see A>. If you loaded it from a fixed disk, you will see C>. This letter and symbol combination is called the *DOS prompt*. Whenever the cursor is positioned immediately after the prompt, DOS is ready to accept a command.

```
Current date is Tue  7-14-1987
Enter new date (mm-dd-yy):
Current time is  3:51:46.14
Enter new time:

The IBM Personal Computer DOS
Version 3.30 (C)Copyright International Business Machines Corp 1981, 1987
               (C)Copyright Microsoft Corp 1981, 1986

A>
```

FIGURE 2-1   The DOS sign-on screen on the IBM PC

If your system has a fixed disk and has been in use for awhile by other people, your DOS prompt may look somewhat different. As you will see later in this book, you can tell DOS exactly what style of prompt you want. Thus, if your prompt differs, don't worry about it.

YOUR FIRST COMMAND

By now you are probably eager to use DOS, so now type **DIR** followed by ENTER. This causes the file directory to be displayed on the screen. You will learn all about files and directories in the next chapter, but essentially, a file is a collection of related information. The directory is a list of all the files contained on the diskette. All files have names, so when you tell DOS to display the directory, it responds by printing the list of file names. File and the directory are analogous to file folders inside a file cabinet.

Because there are more files on the disk than there are lines on the monitor, the first part of the list scrolls off the top of the screen. Don't worry about this — it's completely normal and is exactly what is supposed to happen. Later you will learn ways to control how information is displayed. If you loaded DOS from a diskette, then your screen will be very similar to, or identical to, the screen shown in Figure 2-2. If you loaded DOS from a fixed disk, then you may see different file names than are shown here.

Notice that once the directory has been listed, DOS returns the prompt to the screen. Whenever DOS finishes a command, it redisplays the prompt. This lets you know that it has completed the task. When DOS is accessing a diskette, the small red *drive-active* light comes on. Never remove a diskette from the drive when this light is on; if you do, you might destroy some of the information on the diskette.

The directory listing includes the following items from left to right: the name of the file, the size of the file (in bytes), and the date and time the file was created. We will discuss these items in the next chapter.

Besides listing the directory, the DIR command does two other things. First, it counts the number of files on the diskette. Second, it tells you the amount of free space on the diskette. The amount of storage capacity of a diskette or of a fixed disk varies greatly; you should consult your owner's manual for specific information.

One final point: As stated earlier, DOS does not care whether you enter commands using uppercase or lowercase letters. This book uses

```
GRAPHICS COM     3220   12-30-85   12:00p
JOIN     EXE     8955   12-30-85   12:00p
KEYBFR   COM     3291   12-30-85   12:00p
KEYBGR   COM     3274   12-30-85   12:00p
KEYBIT   COM     3060   12-30-85   12:00p
KEYBSP   COM     3187   12-30-85   12:00p
KEYBUK   COM     3036   12-30-85   12:00p
LABEL    COM     2346   12-30-85   12:00p
MODE     COM     6864   12-30-85   12:00p
MORE     COM      295   12-30-85   12:00p
PRINT    COM     8976   12-30-85   12:00p
RECOVER  COM     4297   12-30-85   12:00p
REPLACE  EXE    11650   12-30-85   12:00p
RESTORE  COM     6012   12-30-85   12:00p
SELECT   COM     3826   12-30-85   12:00p
SHARE    EXE     8580   12-30-85   12:00p
SORT     EXE     1911   12-30-85   12:00p
SUBST    EXE     9911   12-30-85   12:00p
SYS      COM     4620   12-30-85   12:00p
TREE     COM     3357   12-30-85   12:00p
VDISK    SYS     3307   12-30-85   12:00p
XCOPY    EXE    11200   12-30-85   12:00p
        39 File(s)      22528 bytes free

A>
```

FIGURE 2-2   The bottom portion of the DOS diskette directory listing

uppercase letters so you can easily distinguish commands, but in actual practice you will probably usually use lowercase letters.

BACKING UP THE DOS DISKETTE

If your system is new and you are in charge of it, then the most important first step you can take is to back up the DOS diskette. Diskettes can be destroyed or lost easily. For this reason it is imperative to have more than one copy of the DOS diskette. If the backup has already been made by someone else, you should still read this section just so you will know how to do it should the need arise.

In general, you should never work with the original DOS master diskette but always with the backup. It is best to keep the DOS master in a safe place so that it is not accidentally destroyed.

The exact backup procedure varies among systems with two floppy disk drives and those with either one diskette drive or a floppy disk drive and a fixed disk. Read the section that applies to the configuration of your computer. (Remember, if you have version 3.30 and are using 5 1/4-inch diskettes, be sure to back up both diskettes by repeating the following procedures for the second one.) Before you begin, be sure to write-protect the DOS master.

Backup with Two Floppy Disk Drives

To begin the backup procedure, type the command **DISKCOPY A: B:** and press ENTER. Just before you press ENTER, the screen should display this:

```
A>DISKCOPY A: B:
```

DISKCOPY is the DOS command that copies the contents of one diskette to another. After pressing ENTER, you will see the following:

```
Insert SOURCE diskette in drive A:

Insert TARGET diskette in drive B:

Press any key when ready . . .
```

Since the DOS diskette is already in drive A, you need only put a blank diskette in drive B and close the drive door. After that, strike any key. Now, DOS will copy the contents of the DOS diskette onto the blank diskette.

DISKCOPY will display some information about what it is doing, but don't worry about it now. Later, you will be able to understand what it means. The copy process takes a few minutes on most computers, so be prepared for this.

After the copy is complete you will see the message

```
Copy another diskette (Y/N)?
```

If you wish to make another copy of the DOS diskette, type **Y** and the copy process will be repeated; otherwise, type **N**. As you will see, there are many DOS commands that require yes or no (Y/N?) responses.

Backing Up with One Floppy Disk Drive

To begin the backup process in a system with only one floppy disk drive, type **DISKCOPY A: A:** at the prompt and press ENTER. Before you press ENTER, the prompt line should look like this if your system has a fixed disk:

```
C>DISKCOPY A: A:
```

It should look like this if your system only has one floppy disk drive:

```
A>DISKCOPY A: A:
```

DISKCOPY is the DOS command that copies the contents of one diskette to another. After pressing ENTER, you will see the following message on your screen:

```
Insert SOURCE diskette in drive A:

Press any key when ready . . .
```

If the DOS diskette is not already in drive A, put it there now and close the drive door. After that, strike any key. DOS will first read the contents of the DOS diskette into the memory of the computer. Once this has been done, you will see this message:

```
Insert TARGET diskette in drive A:

Press any key when ready . . .
```

At this time, remove the DOS diskette from the computer and put the blank diskette into drive A and press a key. DOS will then copy the information it read from the DOS diskette onto the blank diskette.

DISKCOPY will display some information about what it is doing, but don't worry about it now. Later, you will be able to understand what it means. The copy process using only one drive can take a few minutes, so be patient.

After the copy is complete you will see the message

```
Copy another diskette (Y/N)?
```

If you wish to make another copy of the DOS diskette, type **Y** and the copy process will be repeated; otherwise, type **N**.

What to Do if Something Goes Wrong

Once in a while an error will occur when you are copying a diskette, and you will see an error message. Generally this is caused by a faulty target diskette. The first thing you should do is to try the entire process again. Sometimes things will straighten themselves out. If this doesn't work, try a new target diskette. If this still doesn't work, you should seek advice from a co-worker or the supplier of your computer.

Labeling the Copy of the DOS Diskette

Any diskette that contains information should have a stick-on label on it. The label should include the following items:

- A brief description of what is on the diskette
- The copy number
- Your name
- The date

The reason for the description is obvious: You must have some way to remember what is on the diskette. A good title for the DOS backup copy is "DOS backup disk." Since you might want to have several backup copies, using a copy number is a good idea. You can indicate this by calling the first copy "copy: 1," for example. Include the date the diskette was first put in service. This way you will be able to keep diskettes with similar descriptions separate. Finally, it is a good idea to put your name on your diskettes. In large offices, diskettes have a way of getting lost. Your name helps to ensure that your diskette will find its way back to you.

```
DOS backup diskette
copy: 1
return to:  Herb Schildt
Date: 2/28/87
```

FIGURE 2-3   The suggested format for a diskette label

A good layout for the DOS backup label is shown in Figure 2-3. The time it takes to label your diskettes will save you immense headaches in the long run.

Be sure to prepare the label *before* you put it on the diskette. Once the label is on, you should use only a felt-tipped pen to make changes or corrections to it. Using a ballpoint pen or a pencil may result in lost data because of damage to the magnetic surface.

ANOTHER COMMAND

One of the simplest commands in DOS is the VER command, which displays the version number of the DOS program you are using. To see how it works, type **VER**. You will see a message similar to this:

```
IBM Personal Computer DOS Version   3.30
```

RESTARTING DOS

It is not necessary to actually turn your computer off and then on again to cause DOS to be loaded. Pressing the keys CTRL, ALT, and DEL at the same time causes the computer to reload DOS and begin running it. Try doing this now. If you are using DOS 3.30 with 5 1/4-inch diskettes, be sure to put the Startup diskette into drive A. You will have to reenter the correct date and time because, as far as DOS is concerned, the computer was just turned on—it has no way of knowing that it had just been running a few seconds ago.

You are probably wondering why you would want to restart DOS. There are two possible reasons. First, causing DOS to be reloaded also causes the computer to stop whatever it is doing. Therefore, if the computer begins to do something you think it shouldn't, you can always stop this by reloading DOS. In a sense, pressing the CTRL , ALT, and DEL keys is an emergency stop signal. For now, since you don't know much about DOS yet, if you think that you have accidentally done something that you shouldn't have, just reload DOS.

You also may need to reload DOS if a program fails and DOS is unable to display its prompt. Fortunately, because of the high quality of software available today, program failures are rare. However, they still can occur. A mistake in a computer program is called a *bug*. Some bugs are simply annoyances, but others are so bad that they can actually cause the computer to stop running. When the computer stops, DOS cannot run, which means you must restart the computer by reloading DOS. Hopefully you won't have to do this very often.

TURNING OFF THE COMPUTER

When you are ready to turn the computer off, remember to do one thing first: Remove all diskettes from the drives. When the power is shut off, there is a fraction of a second when the electricity stored in the power supply of the computer "bleeds" out. During this time of decreasing power, the electronics in the computer are in an unstable state. Although unlikely, the disk drive could possibly write random information onto your diskette. This could destroy valued data. Most computers today have safeguards built in to prevent this, but no safeguard is 100 percent effective.

THE SUPPLEMENTAL PROGRAMS DISKETTE

In case you are curious, the supplemental programs diskette contains programs that can be run using the BASIC language. Unless you intend to become a programmer, you will never use this diskette.

SUMMARY

At this point you should know how to

- Start the computer and load DOS
- List the directory
- Make a backup DOS diskette
- Use the VER command
- Reload DOS
- Safely turn off the computer

In the next chapter you will learn more about DOS files and directories.

_3_

DOS BASICS

Before you can go much further in your study of DOS, you should understand a few things about how DOS operates. You will learn about file names, file types, and error messages. You will also learn about DOS's internal and external commands and how DOS actually stores information on a disk.

WHAT IS A FILE?

A file is a collection of related information stored on either a diskette or a fixed disk. (For the rest of this discussion, the word _disk_ will refer to both a floppy disk and a fixed disk.) The magnetic media of a disk is essentially the same as recording tape used in an audio tape recorder. The process of placing information onto the disk is actually very similar to making a tape recording. Reading the information from a disk is similar to playing a tape recording.

A disk can hold several files. In a sense, a disk is like a file cabinet, and disk files are like paper files in a file cabinet. For example, the same disk might contain a letter, a mailing list, and a general ledger, each in a separate file. Because they are in separate files, there is no chance that they will become mixed up. Figure 3-1 illustrates the way files are stored on a disk. (As you will see later, file storage is a little more complicated than this.)

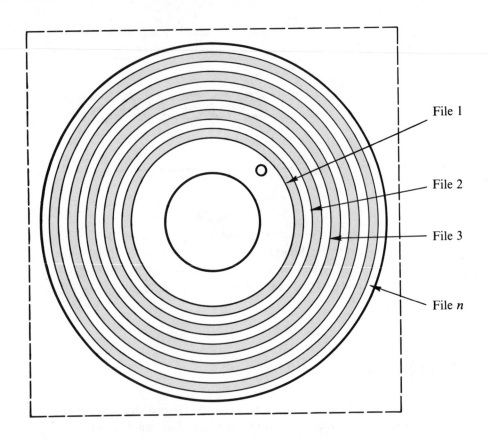

File 1

File 2

File 3

File *n*

FIGURE 3-1   A simplified view of files stored on a diskette

Information is stored on a disk in much the same way that it is stored in memory: byte by byte. (Remember, a byte is roughly the same as a character.) For example, a file might contain the sentence "This is a test." The individual characters that make up that sentence are stored on the disk.

The single most important fact you should know about disk files is that they are concrete, physical entities. They are as real as paper files. Anything you can do with a paper file can be done with a disk file. This includes copying it, changing it, adding to it, changing its name, and unfortunately, losing it. If you keep this fact in mind, you will have no trouble running DOS.

FILE NAMES

Each file on a disk must have a unique name to identify it. A file name can consist of two parts. The first part, traditionally called the *filename,* is essentially what you will think of as the name of the file. It may be from 1 to 8 characters long. The second part of a file name is called the *extension,* and it is optional. The extension exists to help create groups of similar files or to distinguish two files with the same filename from one another. The extension may be up to three characters long. In a way, the filename is like a person's first name and the extension is like a person's last name.

List the directory of the DOS disk at this time. (At the DOS prompt, enter **DIR** followed by ENTER.) See how each name has two parts? For example, one file name is SORT EXE. The filename is SORT and the extension is EXE. Although the directory listing uses one or more spaces to separate the filename from its extension, when you specify a file name you must place a period between the two parts of the name. For example, to tell DOS about the file SORT EXE, you would type **SORT.EXE**. There can be no spaces in the name.

In general, most file names are made up of letters and the digits 0 through 9. However, the only characters that cannot be used in a file name are

. " / \ [ ] : | < > + = ; ,

Also, control characters are not allowed. (A control character is generated by holding down the CTRL key and pressing another key. You will learn more about these characters later.)

THE DIRECTORY

The directory of a disk is a little like the table of contents of a book: it tells what the disk contains. The directory lists the names of the files and

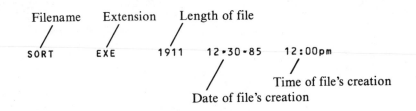

FIGURE 3-2   The parts of a directory listing

each file's length and time and date of creation. A directory is illustrated in Figure 3-2.

The length of the file is shown in bytes. A file to hold the sentence "Hi there." is 9 bytes long. (As far as the computer is concerned, a space is a character, so it has to be counted.) The time and date indicate either when the file was first created or when it was last altered.

Each directory listing begins with two lines of information. If you list the directory of the DOS diskette in the A drive, these two lines will appear:

```
Volume in drive A has no label
Directory of A:\
```

Don't worry about trying to make sense of this now. Later you will understand what it means.

All files listed in the directory must have unique names. Two files with the same filename and extension will not be allowed.

FILE TYPES

Three types of files can be stored on a disk:

- Text files
- Data files
- Program files

Text Files

A text file contains information that you can read. It consists solely of characters that can be displayed on the screen. A common way text files are created is by word processors. In most cases, text files are created and maintained by you. (You will see how later.)

Text files may have any previously unused filename and any extension. However, no text files should use the extension .EXE or .COM because these extensions are reserved for program files.

Data Files

A data file contains information that a program, not a person, can read. Most of the information in a data file cannot be displayed on the monitor because it is in a form only the computer can understand. The special internal representation used by the computer for data is sometimes referred to as *binary* representation of data.

Data files are created and maintained by programs. For example, an inventory management program will create and maintain a data file that holds inventory information.

As with text files, data files may be assigned any previously unused filename and any extension except the extension .EXE or .COM. Many data files use the extension .DAT.

Program Files

Program files contain programs that the computer can execute. Unlike the two other file types, in DOS all program files use either the extension .COM or .EXE. Although there are some differences between program files that use .COM and those that use .EXE, you need to know only that they are both program files and are functionally the same. Program files are created by programmers.

Many of the programs you will use fall into the category of *application programs*. As the name implies, an application program is a program applied to a specific task. For example, a general ledger program is an application program in the area of accounting. In essence, an application program is used to solve a specific problem or to perform a specific task.

Reserved Extensions

DOS reserves a few file name extensions for special purposes, as .EXE and .COM are reserved for program files. For example, the .SYS extension indicates files that only DOS uses. The file extension .BAT indicates a *batch file,* which contains a sequence of commands for DOS to perform. (You will learn how to create batch files in Chapter 8.) The extensions .CPI and .PIF are reserved by DOS for hardware-specific information. Finally, the extension .BAS indicates BASIC program files. It is best not to use any of the reserved extensions in the file names that you create.

OPENING AND CLOSING FILES

When you remove a paper file from a file cabinet, you open the file folder to examine or alter the contents of the file. When you are done, you close the file folder and replace the file in the cabinet. The act of opening and closing a file is paralleled by DOS. Before a file can be used, it must be opened. When the file is through being accessed, it is closed. When a file is open, its contents may be examined or changed. When it is closed, nothing can happen to the file. Whether a file is open or closed is important to you as you use DOS to run application programs.

THE EOF MARKER

All files have a beginning and an end. This seems intuitive and simple enough. But for the computer, knowing where the file stops is not a trivial matter. DOS uses two different methods to determine the end of a file. The first is the *end-of-file*, or EOF, marker. The EOF marker is a special character (CTRL-Z, to be exact) that signals the end of a file. The EOF marker works very well with text files because it is not a printing character. However, with data and program files, the EOF marker is not effective because actual data or program statements might look like an EOF marker, thus making DOS think that the file is shorter than it is. To overcome this situation, DOS uses the length of the file to determine where the end of the file is located.

CHANGING THE CURRENT DRIVE

When you type the DIR command, you get a directory listing of the drive that corresponds to the letter in the prompt. This drive is called the *current* drive. (Sometimes, it is also called the *logged-in* drive.) If you have two floppy disk drives or a fixed disk and a floppy disk drive, you can switch to the other drive by typing its drive letter followed by a colon and pressing ENTER. For example, to switch to the B drive, you enter **B:**. Try this now. (If you loaded DOS from a fixed disk, then try switching to the A drive.) You will see something like this:

```
A>B:
B>_
```

As you can see, the DOS prompt has been changed to reflect the switch to a new drive.

If you have two diskette drives, remove the DOS diskette from drive A and put it in drive B. If you loaded DOS from the fixed disk, place the DOS diskette in drive A. Now enter **DIR**. DOS automatically uses the new drive. In general, all DOS operations occur using the current drive. (It is possible to override this rule, however, as you will see later.)

To switch back to either the A or the C drive, you follow the same format as before, substituting the proper drive designation. Switch back to either the A or C drive now. (If you have two diskette drives, be sure to put the DOS diskette back in drive A.)

INTERNAL AND EXTERNAL COMMANDS

DOS commands are divided into two major groups: internal commands and external commands. An *internal command* is a command that is contained in the part of DOS that stays loaded in the memory of your computer. DIR and VER are examples of internal commands. When you enter an internal command, DOS responds almost instantly. The DOS internal commands are those that you are most likely to need frequently as you use the computer.

An *external command* is not loaded into memory with the rest of DOS; rather, it remains on the DOS diskette. The reason for this is to conserve the computer's memory. DOS includes many little-used commands. Instead of having these consume memory that your application programs could use, DOS leaves them on the disk until they are needed. This means, however, that you can use an external command only when the DOS disk is in the current drive. Also, because external commands are loaded by DOS as needed, there is a slight delay before DOS responds when you use an external command. After an external command has executed, it is no longer kept in memory; it must be reloaded each time that it is used.

DOS's internal and external commands are listed in Table 3-1.

To see an example of an external command in action, enter **CHKDSK**. (Make sure the DOS diskette is in drive A if you don't have a fixed disk.) CHKDSK, short for *check disk,* is an external command that checks the validity of a disk and reports the total space, number of files, and amount of free space on the disk and the total and available amounts of RAM in the computer. CHKDSK displays a list like this:

```
362496 bytes total disk space
 45056 bytes in 3 hidden files
293912 bytes in 39 user files
 22528 bytes available on disk

655360 bytes total memory
604416 bytes free
```

You should have noticed a slight delay before the CHKDSK command was executed. The drive-active indicator light came on, indicating that CHKDSK was being loaded into memory. (If you are wondering about the hidden files, they are some special files used only by DOS, and they do not appear in the directory listing.) You will learn more about the CHKDSK command later.

As you will see in the next chapter, it is easy to copy files between diskettes. If you know that you will need one or more of DOS's external commands, you can copy those you need to another diskette so that you have easy access to them.

Internal Commands	External Commands
CHCP	APPEND
CHDIR (CD)	ASSIGN
CLS	ATTRIB
COPY	BACKUP
CTTY	CHKDSK
DATE	COMMAND
DEL (ERASE)	COMP
DIR	DISKCOMP
ERASE (DEL)	DISKCOPY
MKDIR	FASTOPEN
PATH	FDISK
PROMPT	FIND
RENAME (REN)	FORMAT
RMDIR (RD)	GRAFTABL
SET	GRAPHICS
TIME	JOIN
TYPE	KEYB
VERIFY	LABEL
VOL	MODE
	MORE
	NLSFUNC
	PRINT
	RECOVER
	REPLACE
	RESTORE
	SELECT
	SHARE
	SORT
	SUBST
	SYS
	TREE
	XCOPY

TABLE 3-1   DOS's Internal and External Commands

TRACKS AND SECTORS: A CLOSER LOOK AT HOW DOS STORES FILES

The first part of this chapter provided a simplified explanation of the way DOS stores files on a disk. Although understanding the exact method DOS uses to store a file is not important to using DOS, understanding the concepts behind file storage will help you interpret certain DOS error messages that refer to them. Also, many books, user manuals, and magazine articles assume that you have a basic understanding of the way DOS files are stored.

Information is recorded on a disk in concentric circles called *tracks*. When the disk drive loads a program, you can sometimes hear the read/write head move between tracks. Each track is composed of a number of *sectors*. (The exact number varies and is not important.) Each sector can hold 512 bytes (characters) and is the smallest accessible unit of storage on the disk. (Actually, DOS can use sector sizes other than 512, but it virtually never does.) When DOS records a file on a disk, it does not necessarily use sectors and tracks that are adjacent to each other. That is, DOS may scatter a file throughout the disk's surface. (This is why even a small amount of physical damage to a disk can destroy several files.) This situation is depicted in Figure 3-3.

As mentioned, the smallest accessible unit of disk storage is the sector, which is 512 bytes long. This does not mean, however, that the smallest file is 512 bytes. On the contrary, you can have files of any length from 0 to 64K bytes. However, the full 512-byte sector is allocated to each file, and the rest of the space is not used. (For this reason, several small files can sometimes fill up a disk faster than a few large ones.)

As you can guess, when a file longer than one sector is stored on a disk, there must be some way for DOS to know which sector goes with which file. DOS accomplishes this by storing the location of the first sector of each file in the directory (but you can't see it). Then the location of each subsequent sector in a file is stored in the preceding sector. That is, the directory points to the first sector in a file, and thereafter, each sector points to the next until the end of the file is reached.

The exact position of the tracks and sectors on a disk is determined when the disk is *formatted*. When you made a backup of the DOS master

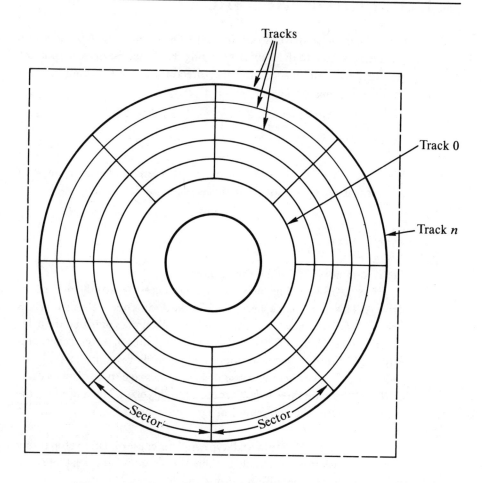

FIGURE 3-3   Sectors and tracks of a diskette

disk, the copy procedure automatically formatted the disk prior to placing information on it. All disks must be formatted before being used. (The
DOS command to format a diskette will be discussed later in this book.)
When a disk is not formatted, DOS and the computer have no way of
knowing where to put information.

A DOS ERROR MESSAGE

Open the door on drive A and enter the DIR command. (If you have a fixed disk, switch to the A drive by typing **A:**.) Since the drive door is not latched, DOS cannot access the disk directory. In a few seconds you will see the following message:

```
Not ready error reading drive A
Abort, Retry, Ignore?
```

If you are using DOS version 3.30 or a more recent implementation, then this error message will look like this:

```
Not ready error reading drive B
Abort, Retry, Fail?
```

Let's examine what this message means.

First, DOS is telling you that it cannot access (read) the diskette in drive A. This is, of course, because the drive door is open. However, DOS does not know the exact cause of the problem; it knows only that the drive is not ready to be used. There are several conditions that could cause this error in addition to the drive door being open. For example, a faulty or unformatted diskette could cause this error message to be displayed.

DOS gives you three ways to respond to this error. You may abort the command, retry the command, or ignore the error. Let's look at these now.

To abort the DIR command, type A. This causes DOS to stop trying to read the diskette. You should use the Abort command when there is no way to remedy the condition causing the error.

The Retry command lets you correct the condition causing the error. To retry the command, close the drive door and then press R. The disk directory will be displayed. Use retry when you can eliminate the error.

The Ignore (Fail) command has limited applications. (Beginning with version 3.30, the term Fail is substituted for Ignore; however, the command's effect is the same.) It tells DOS to ignore the immediate error and continue on with the command. Generally, once one error has occurred, more will follow. The Ignore command is generally used only by programmers because to use it successfully, you need considerable knowledge about how the computer and DOS function.

If you have not done so, close the drive door and press R for Retry. If you have a fixed disk, switch back to drive C by typing **C:**.

DOS ERROR MESSAGES: AN OVERVIEW

In the previous section you saw an example of a DOS error and its associated message. In reality there are several occurrences other than a drive door being open that can cause DOS to issue an error message. As you continue to use DOS you will likely see one or more of these error messages. It is important to respond correctly when presented with an error, so let's take a look at some of the most common errors at this time. (Other error messages will be discussed as the need arises.) Many errors are followed by the prompt

```
Abort, Retry, Ignore?
```

Beginning with version 3.30, the Fail option may also appear. It effectively means the same thing as Ignore. (The slight difference between Fail and Ignore is meaningful only to programmers.)

Bad Command or File Name

The "Bad command or file name" error message is easily the error message you will most commonly see. It tells you that DOS does not understand what you are asking it to do. This message requests no response — you simply reenter the command properly. Generally this message results from misspelling a command. For example, if you type the command DUR instead of DIR, you will see this message.

Disk Boot Failure

In the early days of computers, the initial loading of the operating system was called booting the system. The term *booting* was derived from the phrase "pulling one's self up by the bootstraps." It is used in this sense in the "Disk boot failure" error message, which indicates that the computer could not load DOS from the diskette or fixed disk. If you are using a floppy diskette, replace it with a backup copy. If you are using a fixed disk, you should call a knowledgeable person for help — this message may mean that your fixed disk has failed.

General Failure

The "General failure" error message appears when you attempt to access a diskette that has not been formatted, is damaged, or is not intended for use by DOS or in a DOS-compatible computer. To remedy the problem, either abort the operation or insert a correct diskette and try again.

Insufficient Disk Space

As you know, a disk has only a finite amount of space on it. When you run out of space, you will see the "Insufficient disk space" message. To correct this error, either use a new disk or remove files from the existing disk. (You will learn how to remove files in the next chapter.)

Invalid Drive Specification

The "Invalid drive specification" message appears when you try to specify a drive that does not exist. For example, if you type Z: in an attempt to reach the (nonexistent) drive Z, you will see this message. Simply retry your command with the proper drive letter.

Non-DOS Disk

The "Non-DOS disk" message appears when you try to use a damaged diskette. Usually, it means that the diskette directory is completely or partially destroyed. Either abort your command or retry it with a different diskette.

Nonsystem Disk or Disk Error

The message "Nonsystem disk or disk error" appears when you try to load DOS from a diskette that does not contain it. To correct this error, insert the DOS diskette and strike any key.

Sector Not Found

The "Sector not found" error message is displayed when a sector that is part of a file cannot be found. Because each previous sector points to the next, when a sector is physically damaged, the pointer can become invalid, resulting in this message. Generally, all you can do is try a different diskette. If this error occurs on a fixed disk, then you will have to use a new copy of the file.

Seek

The "Seek" message indicates that the disk drive was unable to find a track. This problem can be caused by three errors. First, the disk drive may be out of alignment — this problem requires a professional technician to repair. Second, the diskette may be improperly inserted in the drive. If so, try inserting it again. Finally, the disk may be physically damaged. In this case, replace the disk.

SUMMARY

You should now understand

- What a file is
- How file names are constructed
- The purpose of the directory
- The differences among text, data, and program files
- How to change the current drive
- The difference between internal and external commands
- What tracks and sectors are
- How to interpret various DOS error messages

Now the DOS basics are behind you. The next chapter teaches you several new and useful DOS commands, including those for copying files, printing the screen, and erasing files.

THE ESSENTIAL
DOS COMMANDS

This chapter presents the core commands that you will need to operate the computer and begin using application programs. At first reading, you may think that there is a lot to remember, but if you work the examples, you will be surprised at how easy it is to keep everything straight. Although these commands just scratch the surface of DOS, they will get you started.

If you do not have a fixed disk, place the copy of the DOS disk that you made in Chapter 2 into drive A at this time. If you are using a 5 1/4-inch version of DOS 3.30 or a later implementation, after loading DOS from your copy of the Startup disk, place your copy of the Operating disk into drive A. (Even if you have a fixed disk, you may place a copy of the DOS master disk in drive A and switch to drive A. Doing so ensures that the examples in this chapter will generally agree with what you see on the screen of your computer.)

Note: This and subsequent chapters present a number of examples, many of which include listings of the DOS disk directory. Since many versions of DOS exist, it is likely that you will have some files not included in the examples, and if you have an early version of DOS, you may be missing a few files. Don't worry about this. The examples shown in the rest of this book will reflect DOS 3.30.

A CLOSER LOOK AT DIR

You learned the simplest form of the DIR command in Chapter 2. However, as you will soon see, DIR is much more flexible. We will take a look at two DIR options.

Two DIR Options

Many DOS commands allow one or more options that alter slightly the meaning or effect of the command. Generally speaking, a DOS command option begins with a slash (/) followed by the specific option. The / signals DOS that an option follows. The DIR command allows two options.

The first DIR option is /P, which tells DOS to temporarily stop listing the directory when the screen is full. Remember that when you listed the directory in Chapter 2, some file names scrolled off the top of the screen. The /P option prevents this. At each pause, you will see the message

```
Strike a key when ready . . .
```

This means that when you are ready for more of the directory, press any key.

To execute the DIR command with the pause option, enter the command line like this:

```
A>DIR /P
```

The first screen should look like that in Figure 4-1.

There are many times when all you want is a list of the files on a disk, and you are not interested in all the other information that DIR displays. When this is your goal, you can use the /W option, which causes DOS to display only the file names in the directory. The file names are displayed in five columns across the screen so that many more file names than usual are visible at one time. To use this option, enter the command line like this:

```
A>DIR /W
```

```
APPEND    EXE     5825    3-17-87   12:00p
ASSIGN    COM     1561    3-17-87   12:00p
ATTRIB    EXE     9529    3-17-87   12:00p
BACKUP    COM    31913    3-18-87   12:00p
BASIC     COM     1063    3-17-87   12:00p
BASICA    COM    36403    3-17-87   12:00p
CHKDSK    COM     9850    3-18-87   12:00p
COMMAND   COM    25307    3-17-87   12:00p
COMP      COM     4214    3-17-87   12:00p
DEBUG     COM    15897    3-17-87   12:00p
DISKCOMP  COM     5879    3-17-87   12:00p
DISKCOPY  COM     6295    3-17-87   12:00p
EDLIN     COM     7526    3-17-87   12:00p
FIND      EXE     6434    3-17-87   12:00p
FORMAT    COM    11616    3-18-87   12:00p
GRAFTABL  COM     6128    3-17-87   12:00p
GRAPHICS  COM     3300    3-17-87   12:00p
JOIN      EXE     8969    3-17-87   12:00p
LABEL     COM     2377    3-17-87   12:00p
MORE      COM      313    3-17-87   12:00p
PRINT     COM     9026    3-17-87   12:00p
RECOVER   COM     4299    3-18-87   12:00p
RESTORE   COM    34643    3-17-87   12:00p
Strike a key when ready . . .
```

FIGURE 4-1   The first screen of the directory using the pause option

The outcome of this command is shown in Figure 4-2. You can remember the /W option as the *wide*-listing option.

Looking for Specific Files

Until now, you have been using the DIR command to list the entire contents of the directory. However, you can use DIR to look for a specific file by specifying its name after the command. You can use this method to quickly determine whether a file is in the directory or not. Try this by entering, for example,

```
DIR DISKCOPY.COM
```

```
A>DIR /W

 Volume in drive A has no label
 Directory of  A:\

APPEND    EXE    ASSIGN   COM    ATTRIB   EXE    BACKUP   COM    BASIC    COM
BASICA    COM    CHKDSK   COM    COMMAND  COM    COMP     COM    DEBUG    COM
DISKCOMP COM    DISKCOPY COM    EDLIN    COM    FIND     EXE    FORMAT   COM
GRAFTABL COM    GRAPHICS COM    JOIN     EXE    LABEL    COM    MORE     COM
PRINT     COM    RECOVER  COM    RESTORE  COM    SHARE    EXE    SORT     EXE
SUBST     EXE    TREE     COM    XCOPY    EXE    BASIC    PIF    BASICA   PIF
MORTGAGE BAS
        31 File(s)       55296 bytes free

A>
```

FIGURE 4-2   A wide directory listing

DOS will display

```
Volume in drive A has no label
Directory of A:\

DISKCOPY COM      6295    3-17-87   12:00p
         1 File(s)       55296 bytes free
```

As you can see, DOS displays information about only the file you request, not the entire directory. (At this time, pay no attention to the volume message; you will learn about it later.)

If you specify a file that is not in the directory you will see this message:

```
File not found
```

For example, see what happens when you enter

```
DIR GARBAGE
```

If you think that the file you requested is really in the directory, you may have made a typing error. If, after a second try, DOS still reports the file as nonexistent, try listing the entire directory; you may have forgotten the file's name.

Wildcard File Names

Up to this point, you have learned how to list either the entire directory or a specific file. However, DOS allows you to list groups of related files. Also, you can list a file without knowing its full name. To accomplish these things requires special *wildcard* characters that can be used in place of an actual file name. Let's see how, starting with an example.

Assume that you want to list the names of all the files on a disk that share the .EXE extension. To do this, enter the following, exactly as shown:

```
DIR *.EXE
```

This causes DOS to display all files with an .EXE extension. The output will be as shown in Figure 4-3.

When used in a file name that is part of a DOS command, the asterisk (*) is a special character that tells DOS to match any sequence of characters. Specifically, it means that any character can occupy the position of the * and all character positions after it. Note that the filename

```
A>DIR *.EXE

    Volume in drive A has no label
    Directory of  A:\

    APPEND   EXE     5825    3-17-87   12:00p
    ATTRIB   EXE     9529    3-17-87   12:00p
    FASTOPEN EXE     3919    3-17-87   12:00p
    FIND     EXE     6434    3-17-87   12:00p
    JOIN     EXE     8969    3-17-87   12:00p
    NLSFUNC  EXE     3060    3-17-87   12:00p
    REPLACE  EXE    11775    3-17-87   12:00p
    SHARE    EXE     8608    3-17-87   12:00p
    SORT     EXE     1977    3-17-87   12:00p
    SUBST    EXE     9909    3-17-87   12:00p
    XCOPY    EXE    11247    3-17-87   12:00p
           11 File(s)     128512 bytes free

    A>
```

FIGURE 4-3   The outcome of the DIR *.EXE command

and extension are separate, so the ∗ applies only to the part of the name in which it is used.

You can use the ∗ to find files whose names have one or more initial characters in common by specifying those characters followed by an ∗. For example, enter this command:

```
DIR S*.EXE
```

DOS will display all files that begin with S and have the .EXE extension—in this case, SHARE.EXE, SORT.EXE, and SUBST.EXE. Note that any sequence of characters may follow the S.

You cannot use the ∗ to find files with filenames that begin with different characters but that have common endings. That is, this command

```
DIR *ST.EXE
```

will *not* find all files with filenames that end in ST. Instead, it will display all files that have the extension .EXE. This is because the ∗ matches any and all characters from its position in the name to the end.

You can use the ∗ in the extension field of a file name. For example, this command

```
DIR S*.*
```

reports all files that begin with S and that have any extension—in this case, SHARE.EXE, SORT.EXE, and SUBST.EXE.

Now try some examples on your own.

The second wildcard character is the question mark (?), which will match any one character in its position. That is, unlike the ∗, it matches only one character—not a sequence of characters. For example, the following command will find all files that end with the characters DISK.

```
DIR ?DISK.*
```

To this command DOS responds with FDISK.COM and VDISK.SYS. (These files are on the Startup disk for DOS 3.30.)

For another example, assume that these files are on your disk:

TEST1A.DAT
TEST2A.DAT
TEST3A.DAT
TEST1B.DAT
TEST2B.DAT

Given the command

```
DIR TEST?A.DAT
```

the files TEST1A.DAT, TEST2A.DAT, and TEST3A.DAT will be displayed.

Now try some examples of your own using the ? wildcard character.

To fully understand the effect of the * and ? wildcard characters, keep in mind that DOS considers the following commands equivalent:

DIR
DIR *.*
DIR ????????.???

All three list the entire contents of the directory.

As you will see later in this book, the wildcard characters are very useful in commands other than DIR because they allow you to easily handle related groups of files.

ANOTHER WAY TO STOP
THE DIRECTORY DISPLAY

The /P option to the DIR command provides a convenient way to stop the directory display, but there is another way, which you will probably use more frequently. If you press CTRL-S , the display will stop until you press another key (or CTRL-S again). The CTRL-S key sequence acts as a toggle that you can remember as stop/start. To try the CTRL-S command, list the directory and then stop the listing at various points.

DOS also lets you stop the display by pressing the CTRL-NUMLOCK key sequence on PC-type keyboards or PAUSE on AT or System/2 keyboards. If you stop the display by using CTRL-NUMLOCK or PAUSE, you must restart it by pressing a different key—these commands are not toggles like CTRL-S. (*Note*: Some PC-compatible computers may behave slightly differently when these keys are pressed.)

Not all application programs that run under DOS recognize the CTRL-S or CTRL-NUMLOCK keys. Therefore, it may not always be possible to stop the display of some programs.

DRIVE SPECIFIERS

In Chapter 3 you learned how to change the current drive by entering the name of the drive you wanted to switch to followed by a colon. This combination of a drive name and a colon is called a *drive specifier*. In addition to changing the current drive, it is used to tell DOS what drive to use for a variety of commands. To see how it works, let's begin with a simple example. If you have two floppy disk drives, insert the DOS disk in drive B, but do not make drive B the current drive. If you have a fixed disk, insert the DOS diskette in drive A, but keep drive C as the current drive. If you have two floppy disk drives, type

```
DIR B:
```

If you have a fixed disk, type

```
DIR A:
```

As you can see, the directory of the drive specified after the DIR command is displayed. The reason for this is that DOS uses the drive specifier to determine which drive is the focus of a command.

For a second example, try this command. (Substitute B: if you have two floppy disk drives.)

```
DIR A:DISKCOPY.COM
```

Again, drive A, not drive C, is searched for the file DISKCOPY.COM.

Again, this occurs because the drive specifier told DOS to look in the A drive for the file.

Although DOS treats all drive specifiers the same, you can think of them as performing two slightly different tasks. First, they tell DOS what drive to use to perform a specific command. This is the case with the DIR A: command. The A: tells DOS to list the directory of the A drive. Second, you can think of the drive specifier as a prefix to a file name as in the second example. For instance, if the file SORT.EXE appears on both the C and A drives, then the file on drive C is referred to as C:SORT.EXE, and the one on drive A is referred to as A:SORT.EXE. In a sense, the drive specifier lets DOS distinguish between files with similar names on different drives.

If you want to enter an external command from a disk that is not the current drive, you can execute it simply by placing a drive specifier before the command name. For example, if you are currently using drive B and CHKDSK is on the disk in drive A, then you would type

`A:CHKDSK`

This will cause DOS to look for the external command on drive A rather than on the currently active drive B.

You will see more uses for drive specifiers as you advance in your understanding and use of DOS.

CLEARING THE SCREEN

It's time to take a little break and look at one of DOS's simplest commands: CLS. CLS clears the monitor's screen. Try this now. As you can see, the screen is cleared, and the DOS prompt is redisplayed in the upper-left corner of the screen.

The CLS command is useful for three reasons. First, you sometimes may have sensitive information on the screen that you do not want everyone to see. When you are done with the information, executing the CLS command is an easy way to wipe it off the screen. Second, occasionally an application program will leave the screen looking "messy." Clearing the screen is a good way to remedy this situation. Finally, if you are not going to be using the computer for a while, it is advisable to clear the screen in order to save the phosphors in the picture tube from undue wear. (The phosphors in a picture tube slowly burn out as they are used.)

PRINTING THE SCREEN

This section assumes that you have a printer attached to your computer. If this is not the case, skip ahead to the next section. If you do not know how to attach your printer to your computer, refer to the installation guide that came with your computer.

It is sometimes very useful to print what is displayed on the screen. DOS lets you do this with the Print Screen command. Unlike most other DOS commands, you do not need to type a special command word—you simply press the PRTSC key. (To reach PRTSC requires the use of the SHIFT key.) To try this, display a directory listing. Once the DOS prompt is displayed, hold down the SHIFT key and press PRTSC. As you can see, the information that is on the screen is printed at the printer.

If you wish to keep a paper record of everything that transpires during a session at the computer, you can do so by pressing CTRL-PRTSC, holding down the CTRL key at the same time as you press PRTSC. Now whatever is displayed on the screen will also be printed by the printer. To stop the continuous printing, type CTRL-PRTSC a second time. The CTRL-PRTSC acts as a toggle: Pressed once, it activates the continuous print facility; pressed again, it deactivates this facility. You should try using CTRL-PRTSC now.

Another way to activate the continuous printing of the screen is to press CTRL-P. Pressing CTRL-P a second time deactivates the printing function.

Formatting Diskettes

Before you can use a diskette to store information, the diskette must be formatted. The formatting process prepares the diskette by setting up the tracks and sectors that DOS uses to store information. The simplest form of the FORMAT command is

FORMAT *drive-specifier*

where *drive-specifier* determines which drive will be used to format the diskette. Note that FORMAT is an external command that must be loaded from disk. This means that the FORMAT command must be on the disk that you are using.

Warning: The FORMAT command must be used with care because the formatting process destroys any data that may already exist on a diskette. If you are preparing a new diskette for use, then there is no data to destroy. However, if you accidentally format a diskette that contains data, that data will be lost forever. Caution: Unless you really know what you are doing, never format your fixed disk. Generally, the fixed disk will already be formatted and will not need to be formatted again. Doing so will irreversibly destroy all files on the disk.

You will need a blank diskette to perform the examples in the rest of this chapter, so let's format one now. If you have two floppy disk drives, insert a blank diskette in drive B and type

```
FORMAT B:
```

If you have a fixed disk or have only one floppy disk drive, type

```
FORMAT A:
```

You will then see the message

```
Insert new diskette for drive A:
and strike ENTER when ready_
```

(If you have two floppy disk drives, the drive specifier in the message will be B:.) If you have only one floppy disk drive, remove the DOS diskette and insert the blank diskette. Once the blank diskette is in the proper drive, press ENTER. The drive will then start, and the formatting process will begin.

When the formatting process is finished, this message will be displayed:

```
Format complete

    362496 bytes total disk space
    362496 bytes available on disk

Format another (Y/N)?_
```

Since you only need one diskette for the examples, answer the prompt by pressing N. The message actually displayed may differ from that shown in two ways. First, there are several different types of floppy drives in use in IBM PC and compatible computers. These drives have different storage capacities. So if the number of bytes of total or available disk space differs, do not worry about it. The message also may differ if part of the floppy diskette was bad and could not be formatted. Although this is not a common occurrence, you are sure to encounter it at some point. If you do, the number of bytes of total disk storage will differ from the amount available, and you will see another line that tells you the exact number of unusable bytes. It is usually best to discard a diskette with bad sectors and use a new one because such a diskette often will deteriorate over time.

In the next chapter you will learn about several FORMAT options that let you control exactly how a diskette is formatted.

AN INTRODUCTION TO THE COPY COMMAND

COPY is one of the most important DOS commands because it lets you make a copy of a file. The COPY command is very powerful. We will look only at its most common use here.

The basic form of the COPY command is

COPY *source-filename destination-filename*

You can remember this format as

COPY *from to*

The COPY command copies the contents of the first (source) file to the second (destination) file. You can also use the COPY command to make multiple copies of a file (but with different names, of course) on the same disk and to copy a file to another disk. For example, the following command copies the file SORT.EXE to the file SORT2.EXE on the same disk.

```
COPY SORT.EXE SORT2.EXE
```

Try this now. As the COPY command begins execution, the disk drive will start, and the drive-active light will be lighted. After the DOS prompt returns, give the following command:

```
DIR SORT*.EXE
```

DOS will respond with the files SORT.EXE and SORT2.EXE. You should notice that the lengths and dates of the files are the same. In fact, the only thing that differs between them is the file name — the contents of the files are identical. When you make copies of an audio tape, the quality of each copy is progressively diminished, but a copy of a disk file is *exactly the same as the original.* In fact, the millionth copy is still exactly the same as the original, so you need have no fear of a file degenerating through the copy process. (It is possible, of course, that a computer failure could cause the copy process to fail, but such an occurrence is fairly rare, and DOS will report it so that you can try again.)

Probably the most common use of the COPY command is to copy a file to another disk for backup purposes. In general, you will always want at least two (three or four are much safer) copies of important files in case one should become destroyed. Assuming that you have at least two drives in your computer, copying a file to another disk is an easy process. The COPY command allows you to specify the disk drive of both source and destination files by using their drive specifiers. For example, if you have a fixed disk and a floppy disk drive, you copy SORT.EXE from the fixed disk to the floppy diskette by entering this command:

```
COPY SORT.EXE A:SORT.EXE
```

To copy from drive A (the current drive) to drive B, you would type

```
COPY SORT.EXE B:SORT.EXE
```

If you only have one disk drive, you can use the form of the COPY command just given, but you will have to swap diskettes in and out as prompted.

If you have two floppy disk drives, put the diskette that you formatted earlier in drive B. If you have a fixed disk, then put the formatted diskette in drive A. Try the appropriate command for your system configuration at this time. Once the copy has been made, list the directory of the destination diskette. You will see that the file SORT.EXE is present on the diskette.

Frankly, the command shown to copy SORT.EXE is seldom used in practice because a shorter form exists. When the destination file is going to have the same name as the source file, only the destination-drive specifier need be used — there is no need to specify the file name again. For example, this command will also copy SORT.EXE.

```
COPY SORT.EXE A:
```

The only time that you will need to specify a name for the destination file is when it will not be the same as the source file name.

Using Wildcards with COPY

It is very common to want to copy several files from one disk to another. Although you could copy each file separately, often you can use the wildcard characters to copy several at once. To see how this works, let's first begin with an example. Try the following command, adjusting the drive specifiers to suit your system. (As the command is shown, it will work for fixed disk systems.)

```
COPY *.EXE A:
```

This command tells DOS to copy to the A drive all files with the .EXE extension. During the copy process, DOS prints on the screen the name of each file copied. A directory listing of the target diskette wil show the following .EXE files (remember, if you are using a version of DOS earlier than 3.30, a different number of files will be displayed):

```
ATTRIB.EXE
FIND.EXE
JOIN.EXE
REPLACE.EXE
SHARE.EXE
SORT.EXE
SUBST.EXE
XCOPY.EXE
```

One of the first things you should notice about the command just given is that the destination file name is missing — only the drive specifier is present. As stated earlier, when you do not specify a destination file name,

DOS assumes that you want the destination file to have the same name as the source file. This same principle applies to wildcard copies: Each file copied to the destination disk has the same name as it did on the source disk. It would be perfectly valid to use the command COPY *.EXE A:*.EXE, but it is redundant.

In general, you can use the ? and * wildcard characters with the COPY command in the same way you use them with the DIR command. If you are unsure as to exactly what files will be copied using a wildcard file name, first execute the DIR command using the same wildcard characters and see what DOS reports.

If you wish to copy all the files listed in the directory of one disk to another, you use the wildcard characters *.*. For example, to copy the contents of the diskette in drive A to the diskette in drive B, type the following command (assuming that A is the current drive):

```
COPY *.* B:
```

You can use COPY to copy files between two disk drives even though neither is the current drive. For example, if you have a fixed disk and two floppy disk drives and the current drive is C, you can transfer the file SAMPLE.CPY from the A drive to the B drive by entering this command:

```
C>COPY A:SAMPLE.CPY B:SAMPLE.CPY
```

Although this may seem obvious, it must be stated: You cannot copy a file onto itself. That is, a command such as this is invalid:

```
COPY TEST TEST
```

Also, if you try to copy a file that does not exist, DOS will display this message

```
File not found
```

At this point you should be able to copy files between disks without any trouble. If you do not feel confident, try some examples before continuing. Later in this book you will learn that the COPY command has several more features and options that make it one of the most powerful DOS commands.

CREATING A SHORT TEXT FILE

Before you can go much further in your study of DOS, you need to have available a short text file. The method that we will use to create a text file is not the one you will normally use to create text files, but it is easy and it will work for now. First, if you are using a fixed disk, make sure that your current drive is C. If you are using a floppy disk drive, make sure that the current drive is A. Enter the following command:

```
COPY CON: TEST
```

This is a special form of the COPY command that causes whatever you type at the keyboard to be written to the file called TEST. (Don't worry too much about this now; it is just a way to create a text file. You will learn more about COPY later.) Next, enter the following lines:

```
This is a sample
text file.
```

Be sure to press ENTER after the period. Now hold down the CTRL key and strike Z. This tells DOS to stop the copy process. After pressing CTRL-Z , press ENTER. Your screen should look like this.

```
C>COPY CON: TEST
This is a sample
text file.
^Z
        1 Files(s) copied
C>
```

(If you have a word processor that you already know how to use, then feel free to employ it to create this text file.)

If you enter the command DIR TEST, you will see that TEST is in the directory, and that it is 30 bytes long.

THE TYPE COMMAND

Now that you have created a text file, you can use the DOS TYPE command to display its contents on the screen. For example, try this command now.

TYPE TEST

This command displays the two lines that you previously entered.

In general, you can use the TYPE command to list on the screen the contents of any text file. (Actually, TYPE can list any sort of file, but only text files will display meaningful information.) The sample file that you used is very short; longer text files will quickly scroll off the screen unless you stop them. You can freeze the display by using the same control keys that you used earlier to stop the DIR command: either CTRL-S or CTRL-NUM LOCK or PAUSE.

An important point to remember is that DOS has no way of knowing which files are text files. That is, as far as DOS is concerned, a file is a file, and text, data, and program files all look pretty much alike to it. It is your responsibility to remember which files are which.

Although we won't be using TYPE again for a while, you will find that in actual practice it is one of the most usual DOS commands because it lets you easily peek into a file to see what's in it.

PRINTING A TEXT FILE
ON A PRINTER

Note: This section assumes that you have a printer attached to your system and that it is attached in the standard fashion. If this is not the case, you should still read this section, but do not try the examples. If you have a specialized printer, contact a co-worker or other knowledgeable person to find out how to print files on it.

When you wish to make a hard copy of a text file, you can do so by using the PRINT command. PRINT is an external command, so you will need to have the DOS diskette available. The simplest form of PRINT is

PRINT *filename*

where *filename* is the name of the text file to be printed. For example, enter this command now.

PRINT TEST

When the PRINT command begins, you will see the message

`Name of list device [PRN]:_`

The DOS PRINT command allows some flexibility in how a printer is attached to your system. (We will look at this and other options later in this book.) However, if your computer is connected in the standard way, you should simply press ENTER. You will then see these messages:

`Resident part of PRINT installed`

`    C:\TEST is currently being printed`

The first message tells you that the part of the PRINT command that communicates with your printer is now loaded into memory. If you execute the PRINT command again, you will not see the initial prompt because DOS will remember what to do. (If the computer has been turned off, then you will, of course, have to respond to the initial prompt again.) The second message informs you that the file TEST is being printed.

You can use a drive specifier in the file name to print a file that is not on the current disk. For example,

`PRINT B:TEST`

prints the file TEST that is found on drive B.

Although TEST is a very short file, you should notice that the DOS prompt returns before the printing has finished. The PRINT command is one of the few DOS commands that runs in *background mode*. This means that you can print a file while using the computer to do something else. This is a very convenient feature. A background task is a very simple form of *multitasking,* in which the computer performs two (or more) operations at essentially the same time.

Canceling a Printout

Suppose that you are in the middle of printing a long file, and you decide that you don't need the printout. To cancel the PRINT command, enter the following:

`PRINT /T`

The /T is a PRINT command option; /T stands for *terminate*.

Printing Multiple Files

You can give PRINT a list of files to print. You can do this in two ways. First, you can execute the PRINT command repeatedly, specifying one file at a time, or you can specify a list of files all at once. To see how this works, copy the file TEST into the files TEST1, TEST2, and TEST3. Now execute this PRINT command.

```
PRINT TEST TEST1 TEST2 TEST3
```

PRINT will respond as follows:

```
A:\TEST is currently being printed
A:\TEST1 is in queue
A:\TEST2 is in queue
A:\TEST3 is in queue
```

PRINT creates a queue of the files you want printed and then prints them one at a time in the order they are specified. (A queue is a list.) Using the DOS default setting, you can queue up to 10 files.

If you decide that you need to print a file called TEST4 while the other files are still being printed, you can add it to the print queue by entering

```
PRINT TEST4
```

This will cause TEST4 to be added to the list of files to be printed.

Removing Files from the Print Queue

Suppose that you have just specified a list of files to be printed, and you decide that one of the files doesn't need to be printed after all. You can remove a specific file from the queue using the /C PRINT option. To remove a file from the queue, use the general form

PRINT *file-name*/C

For example, to remove TEST2 from the print queue, enter

```
PRINT TEST2/C
```

When removing a file, be sure to use its full name. For example, if the file is called SAMPLE.WP, then you must enter

```
PRINT SAMPLE.WP/C
```

to remove it from the queue. Also, if you used a drive specifier with the file name when you added it to the queue, then you must use the same drive specifier when you remove it from the queue.

If you wish to cancel the printing of all files, the easiest way is simply to use the /T option. This terminates the PRINT command and removes all files from the queue.

You should experiment with the PRINT command at this time.

REMOVING FILES FROM A DISK

Often you will only need a file for a short period of time, or you might want to put a disk to a different use and need to remove those files that no longer relate to the new task. Either way, it is a simple matter to remove a file from a disk by using the ERASE command. DOS allows a second name for ERASE called DEL, but this book will continue to use ERASE (you can use whichever form you like). The general form of the ERASE command is

ERASE *name*

where *name* is the name of the file to be erased.

To see how this works, execute this command:

```
COPY TEST TEST2
```

(TEST is the name of the file created in the previous section. If you have not created it, do so now; then execute COPY.) This command causes DOS to make a copy of TEST called TEST2. You can verify that the copy was actually made by using the DIR command.

To erase TEST2 enter

`ERASE TEST2`

You can verify that TEST2 is no longer present by entering

`DIR TEST2`

DOS will respond with

`File not found`

which means that the file no longer exists on the disk.

You can erase all files in the current directory with the command

`ERASE *.*`

DOS will prompt you with the message

`Are you sure (Y/N)?`

If you do want to erase all the files in the current directory, enter **Y**; otherwise, enter **N**.

When you erase a file, you should consider it permanently and irreversibly gone. Contrary to what you might read in various magazine advertisements, it is virtually impossible to recover a file once it has been erased. (In fairness, if you are a top-notch programmer and know exactly what you are doing and — this is important — if you try to recover the file immediately after erasing it, you can sometimes be successful, but this requires the use of special programs not supplied with DOS.) So the rule is to be very careful what you erase, because once a file is gone, it's gone.

CHANGING FILE NAMES

You can change the name of a file by using the RENAME command. DOS allows a short form of this command called REN; however, this book will use RENAME to avoid confusion. The general form of the command is

RENAME *old-name new-name*

You can use RENAME to alter any part of a file's name, including the extension.

For example, try this command (this command assumes that you have the file TEST on the current disk):

```
RENAME TEST RALPH
```

Once the DOS prompt returns, execute the DIR command. You will see that the file TEST is no longer in the directory, but the one called RALPH is. By typing **RALPH**, you can be assured that the contents of the file are the same; only the name has changed.

Since RALPH is a pretty silly name for a file, use RENAME to change it to SAMPLE.TXT by entering this command.

```
RENAME RALPH SAMPLE.TXT
```

You can use drive specifiers with the RENAME command. For example, the following command changes the name of the file TEST to OLDTEST on the B drive.

```
RENAME B:TEST B:OLDTEST
```

If you try to rename a file to a file name that already exists, or if you try to rename a file that does not exist, DOS will respond with the message

```
Duplicate file name or File not found
```

CANCELING A COMMAND

Sometimes you will enter a command, change your mind, and want to cancel the command. Many, but not all, DOS commands can be canceled by pressing CTRL-C or CTRL-BREAK. For many purposes, CTRL-C and CTRL-BREAK are equivalent but in some situations CTRL-BREAK is more effective. For this reason, you should generally use CTRL-BREAK. To try canceling a command, execute DIR and then press CTRL-BREAK before the directory listing has finished. As soon as you press CTRL-BREAK, the screen displays ^C (short for cancel), and the DOS prompt returns. Try this now.

As stated, not all DOS commands can be canceled in this way. For example, because the PRINT command runs as a background task, you must use the /T option to stop it. Also, most commands cannot be canceled in the middle of their execution. That is, most DOS commands have a point of no return. After this point, you cannot stop the command from proceeding. For example, once the RENAME command has begun to actually change a file name, you cannot cancel it until it is done. In more technical language, most DOS commands have a *critical section* that, once entered, cannot be aborted because doing so would corrupt the structure of the disk. You don't need to worry about destroying anything by trying to cancel a command because DOS will not let you cancel at an inappropriate time.

SUMMARY

In this chapter you learned how to

- More fully utilize DIR
- Use wildcard file names
- Freeze the display
- Use drive specifiers
- Clear and print the screen
- Format a diskette
- Copy files
- Display and print files
- Erase files and cancel commands

MORE USEFUL
DOS COMMANDS

This chapter presents some useful DOS commands and examines some of the commands introduced in the last chapter more closely.

CHECKING A DISKETTE
USING CHKDSK

Whether you are using a floppy diskette or a fixed disk drive, the state of the magnetic medium that holds your information is of crucial importance. Unless physical damage is obvious, it is impossible to determine whether the information on a diskette is valid or not simply by looking at it. To verify that the magnetic information on a disk is correct requires the use of a computer and the special command CHKDSK. The CHKDSK command gives you a status report on your disk. CHKDSK is an external command, so you will need to have a copy of it on the disk that is in the current drive. To execute the simplest form of this command, simply enter **CHKDSK** at the DOS prompt followed by ENTER. For example, assuming that the DOS diskette is in drive A, the command

```
A>CHKDSK
```

```
A>chkdsk

   362496 bytes total disk space
    45056 bytes in 3 hidden files
   294912 bytes in 39 user files
    22528 bytes available on disk

   655360 bytes total memory
   609360 bytes free

A>
```

FIGURE 5-1   The output of the CHKDSK command

produces the output shown in Figure 5-1.

As you can see, the CHKDSK command reports the number of bytes of total disk space, the number of bytes used by DOS's hidden files, the number of bytes used by user (accessible) files, and the amount of storage space still available on the diskette. The hidden files are part of DOS and do not show up in the directory listing. The term *user file* refers to a file that the user can display and manipulate. CHKDSK reports both the total system memory and the amount of free memory. The difference between the total free memory and the total system memory is the amount of memory used by DOS itself. CHKDSK also reports the disk volume label, if one is defined, as well as the amount of disk space used by directories and bad sectors.

Disk Errors

Aside from actual physical damage, a disk may become partially unusable for either of two reasons. First, an application program could have an error in it that causes that part of the disk to become detached from the directory. Second, a system fault or unplanned power loss may cause the links between the sectors that comprise the disk to contain incorrect values. In most cases, these types of errors can be detected and corrected by CHKDSK, although information may be lost. In CHKDSK's default mode, presented earlier, errors are detected but not corrected. To make CHKDSK correct errors, you need to specify the / F (Fix) option after the CHKDSK command. For example,

```
CHKDSK /F
```

will cause any error detected to be fixed (if possible).

One of the most common errors you will encounter is reported with this message:

```
X lost clusters found in Y chains.
Convert lost chains to files (Y/N)?
```

where *X* is the number of lost clusters and *Y* is the number of chains. Recall from Chapter 2, that DOS organizes files into sectors, with each sector pointing to the next. A *cluster* is a group of sectors that are all in one track, and a *chain* is a group of clusters. If a cluster becomes disassociated from the directory, then it is said to be lost because DOS no longer knows what file it belongs to. What CHKDSK does with this space is up to you. If you answer yes to the question in the error message, then new files composed of the lost clusters will be created. They will be called by file names of the form FILE*num*.CHK, where *num* is the number of the file. The files will be numbered 0 through 999. In theory, you can examine these files to determine whether they contain useful information; if they do not, erase them. In practice, however, these files seldom contain information that is usable and, even if they do, in most cases you won't be able to tell simply by looking at the file. For these reasons, you should generally answer no to the prompt. CHKDSK will then free the space for future use.

You should run CHKDSK frequently to make sure that your disk is in good working condition. Once a day is normally sufficient unless you have reason to suspect that an error has occurred.

Remember, CHKDSK can clean up certain types of disk errors, but it can do nothing to help a disk that has been physically damaged.

BACKING UP A DISKETTE

Just as you made a backup copy of the DOS master diskette in Chapter 2, you can make backup copies of any diskette using DISKCOPY. The general form of the DISKCOPY command is

```
DISKCOPY source-drive destination-drive
```

For example, to copy the contents of the diskette in drive A to the one in drive B, enter

```
DISKCOPY A: B:
```

If the destination diskette is not formatted, DISKCOPY will format it prior to copying the source diskette. The formatting process does increase the time it takes to copy a diskette, however, so it is often helpful to have a number of formatted diskettes on hand.

If you have only one floppy disk drive, you should use this form of the DISKCOPY command:

```
DISKCOPY A: A:
```

Technically, you can omit either the destination drive specifier or both drive specifiers, because DISKCOPY will use the current drive by default. However, it is safer to fully specify the drive specifiers to avoid any misunderstanding.

DISKCOPY may not be used to copy to or from a fixed disk. However, you can still use floppy diskettes created using DISKCOPY on a system that has a fixed disk.

As stated earlier in this book, several different types of diskettes and disk drives are in use, and these all have different storage capacities. The general rule for applying DISKCOPY is this: The capacity of the source diskette must be smaller than or equal to the capacity of the destination diskette. If this is not the case, DOS will issue a warning message. Generally, you need not worry when you are simply backing up a diskette that was created on the system that is performing the backup.

It is important to understand that DISKCOPY creates an exact copy of the source diskette. That is, sector by sector, the source diskette and the destination diskette are exactly the same. On the other hand, executing a

COPY *.* command will copy all the user files, but the resulting destination diskette, although containing the same files, will not be a duplicate of the original. Most of the time this difference does not matter, but later in this book you will see that there are some special situations in which one method of copying the contents of a diskette is more desirable than the other. For now, however, when you want to copy an entire diskette, you should use DISKCOPY.

Although several things can go wrong during the disk copy process, fortunately they seldom do. If an error does occur, your course of action is determined by the nature of the error. If DISKCOPY reports an error *reading* the source diskette, you should abort the DISKCOPY command and try a different diskette, if a duplicate is available. If a duplicate diskette is not available, try removing the source diskette from the drive and reinserting it. Sometimes a diskette is simply misaligned in the drive. As a last resort, tell DOS to ignore the error and continue. This may lead to the loss of data, however. If DISKCOPY reports an error *formatting* or *writing* the destination diskette, start over again with a new diskette.

DISKCOPY offers the / 1 option, which causes it to copy only one side of a diskette, even if the diskette is double sided. Using both sides of a diskette effectively doubles the storage capacity. Virtually all disk drives in service today are double sided, but the original drives issued when the first IBM PCs came out were single sided. You will use the / 1 option only when you need to copy a single-sided diskette to a double-sided diskette. Most likely you will never need this option.

If you purchase a program, the diskette it comes on may be copy protected. Copy protection prevents the unauthorized duplication of programs. In general, you cannot use DISKCOPY to copy a copy-protected diskette.

When to Back Up Diskettes

Although you are very new to DOS, it is never too early to learn about the importance of backing up diskettes. When you made the backup copy of the DOS system master in Chapter 2, it was to protect the original from harm. This concept can be generalized. Whenever you have valuable data on a diskette, you should make one (or more) copies in case the original diskette is lost, destroyed, or accidentally erased.

Most computer professionals, such as programmers, systems analysts, and maintenance personnel, recommend a system of rotating back-ups. In this method, you create one master diskette and two backup diskettes: a primary and a secondary. At the end of each work period in which the master diskette is altered, the master diskette is copied to the primary backup diskette. Periodically — weekly, for example — the master diskette is copied to the secondary backup diskette. Finally, occasionally — monthly, for example — the secondary diskette is "retired" and put in a safe place. A new secondary backup diskette is then created. In this way you reduce the chances of losing important information. Later in this book, we will look at the backup and protection of diskettes in greater detail.

COMPARING TWO FILES

From time to time you may find yourself unsure whether two files on different diskettes but with the same name are, indeed, the same file. For example, imagine that you have an inventory program that creates and maintains a file called INV.DAT. If you have two copies of this file, how do you know that they both contain the same information? Another related situation arises when you suspect that two files with different names may actually be the same file. How can this be determined? Finally, sometimes you will want to be sure that a file has, indeed, been accurately copied. How can you be sure that the destination file is 100 percent the same as the source file? These are not trivial questions. Although you can type or print text files and visually compare them, some types of files do not lend themselves to visual inspection. The only way to be sure that two files are the same is to use the DOS COMP (Comparison) command. COMP is an external command, so you will need a copy of it on your work disk.

So that you can work along with the examples in this chapter, execute the following command with your work disk in the current drive (or use drive C if you have a fixed disk):

```
COPY TEST TEST2
```

Remember, TEST is the text file created in the previous chapter.

There are two ways to execute COMP. One is simply to enter **COMP**.

You will then be prompted for the two files to compare. As a first example, compare the files TEST and TEST2. The first prompt is

```
Enter Primary file name
```

Respond by entering **TEST**. Next you will see the prompt

```
Enter 2nd file name or drive id
```

Here, *drive id* refers to a file specifier. Respond with **TEST2**. COMP will then compare the files. Upon completion, your screen will look like this:

```
C>COMP

Enter primary file name
TEST

Enter 2nd file name or drive id
TEST2

C:TEST and C:TEST2

Eof mark not found

Files compare ok

Compare more files (Y/N)?_
```

Answer **No** to the prompt.

You should give no special significance to the phrase *primary file*—it really just refers to the first file. As you would expect, since the two files are identical, COMP finds them to be the same. It reports this by printing the message "Files compare ok." Shortly, you will see what happens when the files differ.

You are probably wondering about the message "Eof mark not found." As you learned in Chapter 3, the EOF marker is used to signal the end of the file. However, not all files have EOF markers. When the EOF marker is not present, DOS uses the length of the file to determine the end of the file. Because of the method we used to create the TEST text file, no EOF marker was written; hence, COMP did not find one. Many times, it doesn't matter whether an EOF marker is found or not, but in some special cases it can make a difference. Here's why. As you learned in

Chapter 3, the smallest amount of disk space that DOS can allocate is one sector, which is usually 512 bytes. Even though a file can be as short as one character, it will still require an entire sector to hold it because a sector cannot be subdivided. Some application programs will pad their files to completely fill the last sector. If this occurs, and if the characters used to pad the last sector differ, then COMP could find differences between the two files, even though they are the same insofar as the actual, relevant data is concerned. Thus, if you see the "Eof mark not found" message, the rule of thumb is to not worry about differences between the two files if they only occur at the very end.

Using the Command Line

A much easier way to invoke the COMP command is by specifying the two files to be compared on the command line after the COMP command. For example, to compare TEST and TEST2, use this command line:

```
C>COMP TEST TEST2
```

This form of the command does not prompt you for the file names; it simply performs the comparison.

Keep in mind that when you use the command line form of the command, the files you are comparing must be on disks that are already mounted in the drives because the comparison operation begins immediately. If you must switch diskettes, then use the form of COMP that prompts you for the file names. This will allow you to insert the proper diskettes.

A Comparison Showing Differences

Enter this command:

```
COMP TEST SORT.EXE
```

You will see the message "Files are different sizes," and no comparison will be performed. The COMP command will not compare files that have different sizes because it assumes (rightfully) that different-sized files cannot be the same.

To see what happens when two files of the same length differ, you will need to create a new file that is the same length as the TEST file, but different in content. To do this, enter the following:

```
COPY CON: TEST3
This is a simple
test file.
^Z
```

Since TEST holds the sentence "This is a sample text file." two letters in TEST3 will differ from those in TEST: The *i* in *simple* will differ from the *a* in *sample,* and the *s* in *test* will differ from the *x* in *text.* Now enter this command;

```
COMP TEST TEST3
```

You will see the following output:

```
Compare error at OFFSET B
File 1 = 61

File 2 = 69

Compare error  at OFFSET 14
File 1 = 78

File 2 = 73
```

This rather odd-looking output is telling you that the two files differ in byte numbers 11 and 20. Although hard to believe, it further reports that TEST has an *a* where TEST3 has an *i* and that TEST has an *x* where TEST3 has an *s.* For rather murky reasons, the COMP command reports the position and contents of bytes that differ in *hexadecimal* code. Hexadecimal code is a number system based on 16—a number that computers like. The commonly used decimal number system is based on 10. The hexadecimal digits are the standard digits 0 through 9 plus the letters A through F, which correspond to the numbers 10 through 15. Therefore, the number 10 in hexadecimal format is 16 in decimal format; the number 1A in hexadecimal format is 26 in decimal format. Therefore, the message "Compare error at OFFSET B" means that there was a difference between the two files at character number 11. COMP reports the characters at the point of difference using the internal code used by the computer to represent the character set. For example, hexidecimal 61 (97 in decimal format) is the code for the letter *a,* and hexidecimal 69 (105 in decimal format) is the code for the letter *i.* Frankly, unless you intend to become a programmer, you need not worry about hexidecimal format or character codes. What you do need to understand is that the two files differ; it usually doesn't matter how they differ.

Although the COMP command uses the term *error* when two files differ, this is really not a proper usage of the word. Remember, just because two files are not the same does not mean that one is in error — it just means that they are different. It is certainly possible that the files differ because of an error, but it is not the only nor the most likely reason.

Comparing Files on Separate Diskettes

To try the next example you will need a second formatted diskette. It can be either a blank diskette or a work diskette with some space on it. If you have a fixed disk, place the second diskette in drive A. If you have two floppy disks, put the second diskette in drive B. If you have only one drive, DOS will prompt you to swap diskettes, so have the second diskette ready. Copy the file TEST to the second diskette at this time. To copy TEST from drive A to drive B, enter

```
COPY A:TEST B:
```

It is very easy to compare a file on one disk to one of the same name on another disk. For example, to compare the file TEST on the fixed disk to the file TEST on the floppy disk in drive A, you can enter

```
COMP C:TEST A:TEST
```

Because both the file names are the same except for the drive specifier, you can shorten this command to

```
COMP C:TEST A:
```

Of course, when files are called by different names, you must fully specify both.

A COPY OPTION

You can have the COPY command automatically verify that the file it has just copied is exactly the same as the original without having to actually use the COMP command. Although it is quite rare, occasionally a file copy will not be successful. This can happen for several reasons. By far the most common is a transient power loss or fluctuation that causes the disk drive to temporarily write incorrect data. To guard against this sort of trouble, you can tell COPY to check the destination file against the target file as the copy process proceeds. This will make the COPY operation take longer, but for very important files, this extra time can be worthwhile.

To tell COPY to verify the destination file, you specify the / V option. You enter this option after the rest of the command. For example, to copy with verification the file SORT.EXE from drive C to drive B, you enter this command:

```
C>COPY SORT.EXE B: /V
```

COMPARING DISKETTES

In some situations it may be easier to compare an entire diskette than to compare individual files. For example, if you back up your data diskettes using DISKCOPY, you must compare all files on the diskette to determine whether the backup disk is current. This can be tedious if there are several files. To solve this problem, DOS provides the DISKCOMP command, which compares two diskettes.

If you have two diskette drives, you can easily compare two diskettes by entering this form of the DISKCOMP command:

```
DISKCOMP A: B:
```

You will then be prompted to insert the two diskettes you wish to compare into the drives.

If you only have one floppy disk drive, use this form of the command:

```
DISKCOMP A: A:
```

You will then be prompted to insert the first diskette into drive A. As DISKCOMP runs, it will prompt you to swap diskettes.

If the two diskettes are identical, then DISKCOMP will display the message "Compare OK." If there are differences, DISKCOMP reports the sides and tracks in which the differences occur. Knowing the side and track is not too meaningful (except occasionally to programmers). Generally, though, all you need to know is whether the diskettes are the same.

Just as two files of different sizes cannot be compared using COMP, two diskettes of different capacities cannot be compared using DISK-COMP. As has been mentioned, there are several different types of disk drives in current use. The smallest-capacity diskette holds about 160,000 bytes, and the largest holds about 1,440,000 bytes. Generally, diskettes formatted and used on the same computer will be of the same size, so size is not often a problem when comparing diskettes. However, be prepared for this trouble when comparing diskettes created on different computers.

It is not possible to compare the fixed disk. Even if you have two fixed disks in your system, they cannot be compared.

One particularly good use for DISKCOMP is for verifying that DISK-COPY successfully copied the contents of an important diskette. Although DISKCOPY performs its own error-checking operation, if the data on a backup diskette is extremely important, executing the DISK-COMP command to compare the original diskette and the copy is a very good idea—even if for nothing else than peace of mind.

THE DATE AND TIME COMMANDS

When DOS begins execution, it asks you for the correct date and time, unless you have a clock option installed in your system. However, for one reason or another, the date or the time of the system may not be correct. For example, you or a co-worker may have forgotten to set the time and date. To remedy this situation, DOS provides the DATE and TIME commands.

The DATE command first displays the current system date and then prompts you for a new date, just as when DOS begins execution. Here is an example.

```
Current date is Fri  5-29-1987
Enter new date (mm-dd-yy): _
```

You can either enter a new date or simply press ENTER to accept the original date.

The TIME command displays the current system time and then prompts you for a new time, just as when DOS begins execution. Here is an example.

```
Current time is 16:05:25.57
Enter new time: 10:00:00
```

When using the DATE and TIME commands, remember that DOS uses a 24-hour (military-style) clock. That is, noon is 12:00, 1:00 P.M. is 13:00, and so on. Also, when you enter the corrected time, you cannot enter the tenths-of-a-second position.

Aside from allowing you to change the current system date and time, the DATE and TIME commands are useful when you simply want to know the time of day.

THE DOS EDITING KEYS

Up to this point, when you made a mistake while typing a command, you used the BACKSPACE key to back up to the error and then retyped the rest of the line. Also, if you wished to reexecute a command, you retyped it. In this section you will learn how to use some special keys that will make the entry of DOS commands a little easier. These special keys are called *editing keys* because they allow you to edit (make changes to) what you type on the command line.

Fundamental to using the editing keys is the concept of the input buffer. The *input buffer* is a small region of memory that is used by DOS to hold the commands that you enter from the keyboard. The important point to understand is that the input buffer contains the last command that you typed until you enter a new one. This fact lets you reuse, alter, or fix the immediately preceding command by using the DOS editing keys. The DOS editing keys and their functions are listed in Table 5-1. Let's look at each in turn.

Note that in the remainder of this section you may disregard the "Bad command or file name" error message. Some of the examples in this section will send DOS unknown commands. This hurts nothing, but it does cause an error message to be displayed. Also, this discussion is accurate for the IBM PC, XT, AT, and PS/2 computers. Other types of

Key	Function
F1	Redisplays one character from the input buffer each time it is pressed
F2	Redisplays all characters up to, but not including, a specified character in the input buffer
F3	Redisplays all characters in the input buffer
F4	Deletes all characters up to, but not including, a specified character from the input buffer
F5	Reedits the line you just typed
DEL	Deletes a character from the input buffer
ESC	Cancels the current line just typed prior to pressing ENTER
INS	Inserts the next character typed at the current location in the input buffer

TABLE 5-1   The Dos Editing Keys

computers may use somewhat different keys. You should refer to your user's manual.

The F1 Key

At the DOS prompt, enter **123456789**; then press ENTER. This loads 123456789 into the DOS input buffer. Once the DOS prompt returns, press the F1 key three times. Your command line will look like this:

```
C>123
```

As is obvious from the example, the F1 key redisplays one character at a time from the input buffer. Continue to press the F1 key until the 9 appears. At this point, pressing F1 again has no effect because you have reached the end of the buffer. (DOS does not store the ENTER key in the buffer.) Press ENTER now.

The F2 Key

The F2 key redisplays all characters in the input buffer up to the character that you specify. To use the F2 command, you first press F2 and then the character. For example, if you press F2 and then type **6**, the command line will look like this:

```
C>12345
```

Try this now. DOS redisplays all characters up to the 6. At this time press F1 until the 9 is redisplayed; then press ENTER.

The F3 Key

Probably the most useful editing key is F3 because it redisplays the entire contents of the input buffer. This is especially useful because it lets you reexecute the previous command without retyping it. Press F3 at this time. The command line will look like this:

```
C>123456789
```

Do not press ENTER.

The ESC Key

The cursor currently should immediately follow the 9 on the command line. Press ESC now. As you can see, DOS prints a backslash (\ ) and positions the cursor directly under the 1. The command line will look like this:

```
C>123456789\
  ─
```

The ESC key cancels whatever is on the command line. DOS uses the \ to indicate this cancellation. The DOS prompt is not redisplayed, but the cursor is placed directly under the location it occupied when the prompt was present.

After canceling a command with ESC, you can still use all the editing keys to redisplay or change the previous command. For example, type F3 followed by ENTER.

The DEL Key

To delete a character from the input buffer, use the DEL key. Each time you press DEL, a character will be deleted. You will not see the characters you delete, so use this key with caution. For example, press DEL three times and then press the F3 key. The command line will look like this:

```
C>456789
```

If you press ESC prior to pressing ENTER, you can cancel the effects of the DEL key. Press ESC followed by **F3** and ENTER.

The F4 Key

To delete several characters, use the F4 key. It works somewhat similar to the F2 key in that you first press F4 and then a character. DOS then deletes all characters from the current position up to but not including the character you typed. For example, press F4, type **4**, then press F3. The command line will look like this:

```
C>456789
```

Keep in mind that nothing is displayed when you use the F4 command, so it can be easy to forget what you have deleted; thus, use F4 with caution.

The INS Key

Enter this line at the DOS prompt: **This a test**. Assume that you really wanted to enter **This is a test**. You can correct the command by first pressing F1 to position the cursor after the space that follows *This,* pressing INS, typing **is**, and then pressing F3. When you press the INS key, DOS lets you insert any number of characters at that point without overwriting what is already in the buffer. You should try some examples.

The F5 Key

All the other editing keys let you manipulate the command that is already in the input buffer. Suppose, however, that you began typing a new command and made a mistake. Pressing the F5 key causes DOS to load the input buffer with what you just typed — giving you a chance to correct it — without executing it.

SUMMARY

In this chapter you learned

- How to check a disk using CHKDSK
- How to back up a diskette
- How to compare files and diskettes
- About the TIME and DATE commands
- How to verify files when they are copied
- About the DOS editing keys

In the next chapter you will learn more about DOS's directory structure and subdirectories.

6

SUBDIRECTORIES

Up to this point, you have had only a partial view of how the DOS directory works. We have talked about the directory in the singular, as if each disk could have only one directory. Actually, a disk can contain several directories, with each directory containing a group of related files. In this chapter you will learn how to create, use, and maintain directories.

To follow the examples, format a new diskette now.

ROOT DIRECTORIES AND SUBDIRECTORIES

The directory that we have been working with for the first five chapters of this book is called the *root* directory, and it is the only directory that is guaranteed to be found on a disk. The root directory is created by the formatting process.

You can also define subdirectories of the root directory. A *subdirectory* is more or less a directory within a directory. You can think of the root directory as enclosing the subdirectory. A subdirectory usually holds a group of related files. The exact nature of the relationship is purely subjective. For example, a subdirectory could hold all of a certain employee's files — no matter how divergent in purpose and use those files are. Another subdirectory might hold wage information for all the employees of a company. The point is that DOS doesn't know — or care — how the files are related; it simply treats a subdirectory as a group.

It is common for a subdirectory to have its own subdirectories. In fact, assuming there is sufficient disk space, any directory can contain a subdirectory.

You can think of the root directory as being a filing cabinet with each drawer labeled and used for a specific purpose. The drawers can be thought of as subdirectories. Each drawer (subdirectory) is enclosed by the cabinet (root). Within each drawer, the files can be further organized by topic. This is analogous to a subdirectory within a subdirectory.

It is important to understand that a subdirectory is simply a term used to describe a relationship between two directories. The directory that encloses a subdirectory is called the *parent* directory. The only directory that does not have a parent is the root.

Throughout this chapter and the rest of the book, unless specific clarification is required, the term *directory* will refer to any type of directory — root or subdirectory.

DIRECTORY TREE STRUCTURE

The disk directory structure used by DOS is called *tree structured* because, when drawn in a diagram on paper, the root and subdirectories resemble the root system of a tree. For example, the directory structure of a disk that is used by a small hypothetical insurance office may look like that shown (conceptually) in Figure 6-1.

In Figure 6-1, the root directory contains three subdirectories: word processing, accounting, and games. Word processing, in turn, contains two subdirectories of its own: form letters and temporary letters. The accounting subdirectory contains three subdirectories: A/R (accounts receivable), A/P (accounts payable), and G/L (general ledger). The games subdirectory has no further subdirectories.

The theory and rationale behind tree-structured directories is that related groups of files can be treated as units of increasing specialization. For example, the directory for word processing branches from the root because word processing is a logically separate task from accounting and games. Word processing itself contains two distinct types of documents: reusable form letters and disposable, single-use correspondence. As you

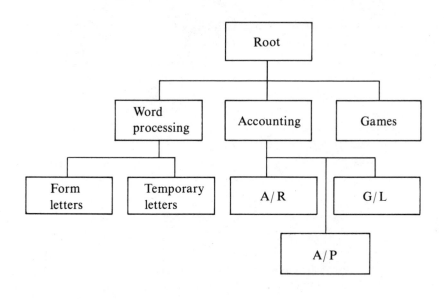

FIGURE 6-1   A diagrammatic form of a tree-structured directory

move down the tree from the root, each directory becomes more specialized in what it contains.

CREATING SUBDIRECTORIES

Before you proceed further in this discussion of subdirectories, you
should create actual examples that you can work with. To gain the fullest
understanding of this discussion, you should work out the text examples
at your computer as we proceed. Place a newly formatted diskette in drive
A and switch to drive A at this time if it is not already the current drive.
(This instruction applies to fixed disk users as well.)

In this section, you will create a disk directory structure that imple-
ments the tree structure shown in Figure 6-1.

To create a subdirectory you use the MKDIR (or MD) command. The general form of this command is

    MKDIR *directory-name*

A directory name must conform to the same conventions and restrictions as a file name except that it may not have an extension. Enter the following command:

```
MKDIR WP
```

Here, WP is short for word processing, which is too long to be a directory name. Once the prompt returns, enter **DIR**. The only entry will look like this:

```
WP          <DIR>   5-30-87    2:58p
```

(Of course, your date and time will be different.) The <DIR> signifies that WP is a directory rather than a file. Keep in mind that you are still in the root directory.

    Before moving on, create the other two directories that branch from the root. Enter these two commands:

```
MKDIR ACCOUNTS

MKDIR GAMES
```

Here, ACCOUNTS is short for accounting. You can list the directory again to see the effect of these commands.

CHANGING DIRECTORIES

Now that you have created three subdirectories, it is time to see how to activate one. The CHDIR (or CD) command is used to change the current directory. Just as you can change the current drive, you can change the current directory. For example, to make the WP directory current, enter

```
CD WP
```

Try this now. (When a short form of a command exists, this book generally uses the long form to avoid confusion. However, since CD is almost universally used instead of CHDIR, it will be used in this book.)

Once the prompt returns, list the directory. You will see this display:

```
Volume in drive A has no label
Directory of A:\WP

    .            <DIR>      5-30-87   2:58p
    ..           <DIR>      5-30-87   2:58p
```

Take a close look at this display. One of the first features you should notice is that the directory name is shown in the line that reads "Directory of A: \WP". If you recall, when you list the root directory, only the backslash is displayed. In DOS, the backslash is used to represent the root directory, which has no name. The combination \WP specifies a *path* to the WP directory. That is, begin at the root and then go to WP. You will learn more about paths a little later.

The two directory entries are represented in DOS shorthand. The single period is shorthand for the current directory, and the two periods represent the parent directory — which in this case is the root directory. For example, if you enter

```
DIR ..
```

the root directory will be displayed. Typing

```
DIR .
```

lists the current subdirectory. Remember, to list the current directory (subdirectory or root), you need only enter **DIR**. The period is redundant.

CREATING SUBDIRECTORIES WITHIN A SUBDIRECTORY

You create a subdirectory inside of a subdirectory in exactly the same way that you created a subdirectory from the root. Let's create the two subdirectories to WP at this time. Enter the following commands and then list the directory.

```
MKDIR FORMLET

MKDIR TEMP
```

In our imaginary insurance office, FORMLET will be used to store form letters, and TEMP will hold correspondence that will be in the system only a short period of time. A directory listing will now look like this:

```
Volume in drive A has no label
Directory of A:\WP

    .           <DIR>     5-30-87   2:58p
    ..          <DIR>     5-30-87   2:58p
    FORMLET     <DIR>     5-30-87   3:20P
    TEMP        <DIR>     5-30-87   3:21P
```

(Again, your date and time will differ.)
Switch to the FORMLET directory by entering

```
CD FORMLET
```

and list the directory. The second line will now look like this:

```
Directory of A:\WP\FORMLET
```

As you might guess, \WP \FORMLET specifies the path to the FORM-LET directory. It is interpreted like this: Start at the root and go to the WP directory; from the WP directory, go to the FORMLET directory. This path is shown in Figure 6-2.

Before continuing, you will need to create a short text file in the FORMLET directory. To do this, execute the COPY command as shown here. (In the next chapter you will learn to use DOS's text editor, which will make the creation of text files easier.)

```
COPY CON: SAMPLE
```

Next, enter the following lines, followed by CTRL-Z to terminate the input process.

```
The summer soldier,
The sunshine patriot
^Z
```

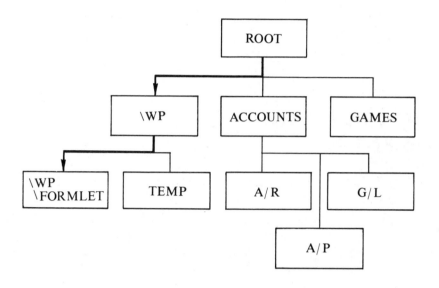

FIGURE 6-2   The path to the FORMLET directory

RETURNING TO THE PARENT DIRECTORY

There are two ways to move from a subdirectory to its parent. The first, and by far the most common, is to issue this command:

CD ..

Since the two periods are shorthand for the parent's directory name, this works no matter what the parent directory is called.

The second way to return to the parent directory is to explicitly specify its name. For example, to go from the FORMLET directory to the

WP directory you can enter

```
CD \WP
```

The backslash is necessary for reasons that will soon become clear.

RETURNING TO THE ROOT DIRECTORY

No matter how deep you are in subdirectories, you can always return to the root directory by entering this command:

```
CD \
```

Because the backslash is DOS's name for the root directory, this causes DOS to make the root directory active.

Of course, you may always return to the root directory by entering repeated CD.. commands until you reach the root.

CREATING MORE DIRECTORIES

If you haven't yet done so, return to the root directory at this time. To continue setting up the directories on the disk, enter these commands:

```
MKDIR ACCOUNTS

MKDIR GAMES
```

Switch to the ACCOUNTS directory and enter these commands:

```
MKDIR AR

MKDIR AP

MKDIR GL
```

PATHS AND PATH NAMES

Each directory has a unique path from the root to itself. For example, the path to the GL directory, beginning at the root, is first to ACCOUNTS and then to GL. In the language of DOS, you specify a path by using a *path name*. The path name for the GL directory is \ACCOUNTS \GL. By using the complete path name you can access any file in any directory, no matter what directory is currently active. For example, to display the SAMPLE file that you created in the FORMLET subdirectory of WP, enter this command:

```
TYPE \WP\FORMLET\SAMPLE
```

The first backslash is DOS's name for the root. The backslash that precedes the file name SAMPLE is necessary and acts as a separator between the path name and the file name. In general, you use backslashes to separate directory and file names. There can be no spaces in the path name.

As another example, try this command:

```
DIR \WP\TEMP
```

You will see the directory of the TEMP directory displayed.

The general form of a path name is

dir-name *dir-name*... *dir-name*

where *dir-name* is an appropriate directory name. For example, if TEMP under WP had a subdirectory called HARRY, then the HARRY directory could be listed using this command:

```
DIR \WP\TEMP\HARRY
```

You may precede a path name with a drive specifier if necessary. For example, to list a directory called SPRDSHT on drive B, you enter

```
DIR B:\SPRDSHT
```

DOS restricts the length of a path name to 63 characters.

MOVING BETWEEN DIRECTORIES

There are several ways to move between directories. One way that will always work, no matter what directory is currently active, is to enter the CD command followed by the complete path name of the directory to which you wish to go. For example, return to the root directory by entering CD \, then move to the WP directory by entering CD WP. Now, to move from the WP directory to the AR subdirectory of ACCOUNTS, you can use this command:

```
CD \ACCOUNTS\AR
```

To return to the WP directory, enter

```
CD \WP
```

Return to the WP directory now.

If you type an invalid path or misspell a directory name, DOS will respond with the message "Invalid directory". In this case, enter the command again, correcting the error.

To move from the WP directory to its TEMP subdirectory, you *cannot* use this command:

```
CD \TEMP        (This is an incorrect command.)
```

(If you try this command, DOS will respond with the message "Invalid directory".) This command will not work because the backslash preceding TEMP tells DOS to start at the root and then move to the TEMP directory. However, TEMP is not a subdirectory of the root—it is a subdirectory of WP. Hence, to move from WP to TEMP, you must use one of these commands:

```
CD TEMP

CD \WP\TEMP
```

The first command is essentially a shorthand version of the second. Because the WP directory is active and TEMP is a subdirectory of WP, you can simply use CD TEMP because DOS already knows the rest of the path. The second form works, of course, because the entire path is explicitly stated. In general, any time you move from a parent directory to a subdirectory, you need specify only the subdirectory name. However, the reverse is not true. To move from a subdirectory back to the parent, you must use either the CD.. command or a complete path name.

DISPLAYING THE CURRENT DIRECTORY NAME

In addition to allowing you to change directories, the CD command also displays the current directory and path if it is executed with no arguments. To try this, enter CD at this time. If you ever have any doubts about being in the proper directory, using this command is the way to find out.

For example, switch to the TEMP subdirectory of WP and enter CD. Your display will look like this:

```
A:\WP\TEMP
```

REMOVING A DIRECTORY

To remove a directory, you must use the RMDIR (or RD) command. Directories cannot be removed using ERASE. There are two restrictions to removing directories. First, the directory must be empty; it can contain no files or other subdirectories. When you list the directory, you should see only:

```
.        <DIR>
..       <DIR>
```

Second, the directory may not be the current directory. That is, you cannot remove a directory that you are currently using.

Switch to the ACCOUNTS directory at this time. Since the GL directory is empty, remove it now by entering

```
RMDIR \ACCOUNTS\GL
```

If you list the directory, you will see that GL no longer appears.

Before continuing, recreate the GL directory.

If you try to remove the current directory or a nonexistent directory, you will see this message:

```
Invalid path, not directory,
or directory not empty
```

COPYING FILES BETWEEN DIRECTORIES

When you copy a file from one directory to another, you must be sure to fully specify the path names. For example, switch to the AR directory of ACCOUNTS and enter this command:

```
COPY \WP\FORMLET\SAMPLE \ACCOUNTS\AR
```

If you list the AR directory, you will see that the SAMPLE file has been copied into it.

Technically, if the destination directory is the current directory, then the destination need not be specified. That is, if AR is the current directory, then the following form of the COPY command also copies the file SAMPLE.

```
COPY \WP\FORMLET\SAMPLE
```

To copy a file from a subdirectory to the root directory, use the backslash as the destination path. For example, the following command copies the file SAMPLE to the root (assuming that the AR directory is current).

```
COPY SAMPLE \
```

Earlier in this book, you were told that no two files on the same diskette could have the same name. Although this statement is true, it needs to be qualified in light of subdirectories. Put more fully, no two files on the same diskette and *sharing the same path name* can have the same name. That is, *within any directory,* no two file names can be the same. However, files in other directories can have similar names. DOS keeps similar names straight because it always associates a path name with a file name.

DISPLAYING A DISK'S DIRECTORY STRUCTURE

DOS provides two commands for displaying the directory structure of a disk. The first is TREE, which displays all directories and subdirectories. The second is CHKDSK used with the / V option. Let's look at both of these now.

The TREE Command

The TREE command displays the names of all directories on the specified disk. The general form of the TREE command is

TREE *drive-specifier*

The *drive-specifier* is unnecessary if you want the structure of the disk in the current drive. TREE is an external command, which means that you must have it on your work disk.

To see how TREE works, copy the file TREE.COM into the root directory of your work disk and enter **TREE**. (Make sure that drive A is active.) You will see output similar to that shown in Figure 6-3.

If you want a list of the files in each directory, use the / F option. For example, the following command lists both the directory structure and files in each directory.

TREE / F

The output from this form of the TREE command is shown in Figure 6-4.

By adding a drive specifier to the path name, you can use TREE to display the directory structure of a disk in a different drive.

```
DIRECTORY PATH LISTING

Path: \WP

Sub-directories:    FORMLET
                    TEMP


Path: \WP\FORMLET

Sub-directories:    None


Path: \WP\TEMP

Sub-directories:    None


Path: \ACCOUNTS

Sub-directories:    AR
                    AP
                    GL


Path: \ACCOUNTS\AR

Sub-directories:    None


Path: \ACCOUNTS\AP

Sub-directories:    None


Path: \ACCOUNTS\GL

Sub-directories:    None


Path: \GAMES

Sub-directories:    None
```

FIGURE 6-3   Output from the TREE command

```
DIRECTORY PATH LISTING

Files:              SAMPLE
                    TREE    .COM


Path: \WP

Sub-directories:    FORMLET
                    TEMP

Files:              None



Path: \WP\FORMLET

Sub-directories:    None

Files:              SAMPLE



Path: \WP\TEMP

Sub-directories:    None

Files:              None



Path: \ACCOUNTS

Sub-directories:    AR
                    AP
                    GL

Files:              None



Path: \ACCOUNTS\AR

Sub-directories:    None

Files:              SAMPLE
```

FIGURE 6-4   Output from the TREE command using the / F option

```
         Path: \ACCOUNTS\AP

         Sub-directories:   None

         Files:             None



         Path: \ACCOUNTS\GL

         Sub-directories:   None

         Files:             None



         Path: \GAMES

         Sub-directories:   None

         Files:             None
```

FIGURE 6-4   Output from the TREE command using the / F option (*continued*)

Using CHKDSK to Display
the Directory Structure

You can use CHKDSK to display a list of the directories and files on a
disk by specifying the /V option. (Remember that CHKDSK is an
external command.) The output is not in the same form—or as easy to
read—as that created by TREE, but it does have the advantage that it
checks the disk and provides other useful information. To use CHKDSK
to display the directories and files, use the following form (remember to
copy CHKDSK.COM to your work disk first):

```
CHKDSK /V
```

The output generated by this command is shown in Figure 6-5.

```
           Directory A:\
                 A:\IBMBIO.COM
                 A:\IBMDOS.COM
           Directory A:\WP
           Directory A:\WP\FORMLET
                 A:\WP\FORMLET\SAMPLE
           Directory A:\WP\TEMP
           Directory A:\ACCOUNTS
           Directory A:\ACCOUNTS\AR
                 A:\ACCOUNTS\AR\SAMPLE
           Directory A:\ACCOUNTS\AP
           Directory A:\ACCOUNTS\GL
           Directory A:\GAMES
                 A:\SAMPLE
                 A:\TREE.COM
                 A:\CHKDSK.COM


           362496 bytes total disk space
            53248 bytes in 3 hidden files
             8192 bytes in 8 directories
            17408 bytes in 5 user files
           283648 bytes available on disk

           655360 bytes total memory
           594976 bytes free
```

FIGURE 6-5   Output from the CHKDSK command using the /V option

(Remember, the exact output may vary slightly, depending upon the version of DOS you are using.)

DIRECTORY CAPACITY

The root directory of a disk can hold a fixed number of entries, depending upon the capacity of the disk. (An entry is either a file or subdirectory name.) Table 6-1 shows the number of entries for the most common diskette formats. The root directory of the fixed disk can hold 512 entries.

Unlike the root directory, a subdirectory can hold as many entries as

Diskette capacity (in bytes)	Maximum number of entries
160/180K	64
320/360K	112
720K	112
1200K	224
1440K	224

TABLE 6-1   Directory Capacity of Various Diskettes

available disk space allows. This is because DOS simply continues to allocate space on the disk to hold the entries. In general, however, you should not have extremely large directories because they are difficult to manage. Once you have more than 100 or so entries, it is time to think about creating a new subdirectory and moving some of the files to it.

MANAGING YOUR DIRECTORIES

Although we will look more closely at the topic of directory management later in this book, a few pointers will be given now. First and foremost, subdirectories should be used to hold logically related groups of files. Files can be related to each other in several different ways. For example, if a computer is shared by a number of people, then creating a subdirectory for each individual is probably a good idea. Even though all the files in a user's subdirectory may be quite different in purpose from one another, they are all related because they belong to that user. However, if a computer is being used by one person for several separate tasks, as in the example presented earlier in this chapter, then the subdirectories are best organized by functional areas. Generally, the way the computer is used should dictate the directory design.

It is important to remember that each subdirectory uses disk space. Creating an unnecessarily large number of subdirectories wastes disk space. Also, subdirectories that are deeply nested and therefore require long path names slow DOS's access time to any files they contain. You must balance these factors against the advantages that subdirectories have to offer.

SUMMARY

In this chapter you learned

- That DOS uses a tree-structured system of directories
- The difference between root and subdirectories
- How to create and remove subdirectories
- How to move between directories
- What a path name is
- How to display the directory structure of a disk using TREE or CHKDSK
- How many directory entries that various types of disks can hold

In the next chapter you will learn to use EDLIN, the DOS text editor.

7

EDLIN: THE DOS TEXT EDITOR

Up to this point, you have been creating short text files using a special case application of the COPY command. While this was sufficient to help you learn about DOS, it is totally inadequate for general use. Instead, DOS provides a text editor called EDLIN which you can use to create and modify text files.

Note: If you have a different text editor or word processor and know how to use it, you may want to skip this chapter because there is little point in learning to use EDLIN if you already have and use a different editor.

You will need your work copy of the DOS diskette to follow the examples in this chapter unless you are a fixed disk user.

WHAT EDLIN IS AND ISN'T

Formally, EDLIN is a line-oriented text editor. It is neither a screen-based editor nor, in the proper definition of the term, a word processor. Its sole function is to allow the creation and modification of text files on a line-by-line basis. As text editors go, EDLIN is of a rather old style. Though it contains no flashy features, it is sufficient.

If you are new to microcomputers, be aware that EDLIN is not representative of the types of text editors in general use. It is a simple editor supplied by DOS to allow you to create and modify short text files that will help you customize and tailor DOS to your needs. It is not intended to take the place of either a full-featured, screen-oriented text editor or a word processor. If you need to perform extensive editing or word processing, you should invest in a high-performance package.

Most current editors use the WYSIWYG (wiz-ee-wig) approach, or What You See Is What You Get — what appears on the screen is the way the file will look when printed. However, EDLIN does not completely follow this principle; how the file looks in the editor will be somewhat different from how it will look when printed.

Another difference between EDLIN and most modern-style editors is that EDLIN does not use the arrow keys to move around on the screen. EDLIN is not screen oriented; instead, it is line oriented, which means that it can only deal with one line of text at a time.

EXECUTING EDLIN

EDLIN is an external command, so you will need a copy of EDLIN.COM on your work disk. To execute EDLIN, use the general form

EDLIN *file-name*

where *file-name* is the name of the text file you wish to edit. If *file-name* does not exist, EDLIN will create it. If you do not specify a file name, DOS tells you that you must do so. Remember that the *file-name* may include a drive specifier and a path name.

SOME EDLIN BASICS

In this section you will learn some of the essentials of EDLIN's operation, including entering text, listing the file, saving the file, and exiting EDLIN. EDLIN's commands will be discussed in detail later in this chapter.

Creating a Text File

Execute EDLIN by entering

```
EDLIN EDTEST.TXT
```

When EDLIN begins executing, you will see the following:

```
New file
*_
```

As you expect, the message "New file" simply means that the specified file did not exist and EDLIN has created it. The asterisk (*) is EDLIN's prompt. Whenever you see it, you know that EDLIN is ready to accept a command.

This is an important point: EDLIN operates a little like DOS itself by displaying a prompt and then waiting for commands. Each time you give EDLIN a command, it does what it is told.

Entering Text

As stated, when EDLIN displays its prompt, it is in command mode and is *not* ready to accept text. To cause EDLIN to accept text, you must enter the I (INSERT) command. (All EDLIN commands can be entered in upper- or lowercase, as you like.) For example, press I and ENTER and type these lines of text.

Now is the time
for all good men
to come to the aid of their country.

Your screen will look like this.

```
*I
       1:*Now is the time
       2:*for all good men
       3:*to come to the aid of their country.
       4:*_
```

In insert mode, EDLIN tabs in, displays the current line number and an asterisk (which in insert mode indicates the currently active line), and waits for input. Each time you press ENTER, a new line number is displayed. Please remember that when the asterisk follows the line number, it is not a command prompt but simply an indicator of the active line. (This is one of the most confusing aspects of EDLIN.)

The line numbers are not part of your file and will not be on the disk when the file is saved. Rather, EDLIN supplies them as both a convenience and a means of referring to a line.

If you make a mistake while typing, you can use the same commands, function keys, and control keys that DOS accepts to correct your mistake. However, once you have pressed ENTER, you must use a special EDLIN command to make corrections.

To stop entering text, you must press the CTRL-BREAK key sequence. Try this now. As you can see, a ^C is displayed and EDLIN's prompt returns once more.

Listing the File

To list the contents of the file currently being edited, you use the L (LIST LINES) command. To execute its simplest form, simply press L and ENTER. Do so now. The text you just entered will be displayed like this.

```
1: Now is the time
2: for all good men
3: to come to the aid of their country.
```

Terminating EDLIN

There are two ways to terminate EDLIN. The one that you will use most often is the E (END EDIT) command, which causes EDLIN to save the contents of the file and then terminate. The other is the Q (QUIT EDIT) command, which causes EDLIN to abort without saving the file to disk.

Exit EDLIN by using the E command at this time.

Reediting a File

EDLIN behaves a little differently when you are editing a preexisting file than it does when you are editing a new file. To begin, edit EDTEST.TXT again by entering

```
EDLIN EDTEST.TXT
```

When EDLIN begins execution, you will see the following:

```
End of input file
*
```

The message "End of input file" is EDLIN's way to tell you that it has loaded the entire file into memory. The only time you will not see this message is when (and if) you edit a file large enough that it cannot all fit into memory. In this case EDLIN reads the file until 75 percent of the memory is used, leaving 25 percent for working space. To edit the remainder of a large file, you will need to use some special commands (discussed later) that write part of the file back to disk and read in some more of the file from disk. However, you probably will never have a file larger than will fit into memory.

List the file at this time using the L command. It will look like this.

```
1:*Now is the time
2: for all good men
3: to come to the aid of their country.
```

Notice that the asterisk is at the start of line 1. This is how EDLIN tells you which line is current. The current line determines where certain editor commands will take place. For example, if you enter the I command and begin inserting text, the text that you enter will be inserted *before* line 1. Try this now by entering insert mode and then typing **This is before line one**. Press ENTER and then CTRL-BREAK. List the file. Your screen will look like this.

```
1: This is before line one
2:*Now is the time
3: for all good men
4: to come to the aid of their country.
```

Notice that line 2 is now current. In the next section we will discuss more fully the meaning and manipulation of the current line.

Now enter the E command, which saves the file to disk and exits the editor. At the DOS prompt, enter the following command:

```
DIR EDTEST.*
```

Two files will be displayed. One is EDTEST.TXT, as you would expect because this is the name of the file that you are editing. The other is called EDTEST.BAK and contains the previous version of EDTEST.TXT. The .BAK extension stands for backup. Each time EDLIN saves text to an already existing file, it first renames the extension of the existing file to .BAK and then writes the text to disk using the actual file name. In this way you always have the old version of your file to fall back on if you accidentally corrupt the current version. Periodically, you may want to erase backup files that you no longer need in order to free disk space.

The Current Line

Intrinsic to the operation of EDLIN is the concept of the *current line*. You can think of the current line as being the one you are "on" or "at." As stated earlier, EDLIN identifies the current line with the asterisk. When you first begin editing a file, line 1 is current. As you will see shortly, a number of EDLIN commands change the current line.

When you insert text, it is placed before the current line, and the rest of the existing text is moved down.

EDLIN'S COMMANDS

Now that you know the basics of EDLIN's operation, it is time to study its commands in greater detail. EDLIN has 14 commands, which are summarized in Table 7-1.

Let's look at each of these commands in turn.

Command	Meaning
A	Append lines (from disk file)
C	Copy lines
D	Delete lines
E	End edit and save file
I	Insert lines
L	List lines
M	Move lines
P	Display a page (23 lines)
Q	Quit (does not save file)
R	Replace text
S	Search text
T	Transfer lines (merges one file into another)
W	Write lines (to file)
line-num	Intraline edit *line-num* line

TABLE 7-1   The EDLIN Commands

INSERTING TEXT

At this point edit EDTEST.TXT (use EDLIN EDTEST.TXT). Type **2I** and press ENTER. Type **this is new line two** and press ENTER and CTRL-BREAK. Use the L command to list the file. It will look like this.

```
1: This is before line one
2: this is new line two
3:*Now is the time
4: for all good men
5: to come to the aid of their country.
```

By placing a line number in front of the I command, you told EDLIN to begin inserting text immediately before that line. The general form of the I command is

*line-num*I

where *line-num* is the number of the line you wish to begin adding text in front of. If you don't specify the line number, text is inserted before the current line.

To add text to the end of a file, simply specify a line number that is greater than the last line number of the file. For example, to add lines to the end of the EDTEST.TXT file, you can enter **6I**. Try this now. Add the lines

Text editors
are fun to use
as long as you know the
right commands.

and then press CTRL-BREAK. If you list the file, you will see that the lines have indeed been added to the end.

DELETING LINES

To delete lines of text, use the D (DELETE LINES) command. The DELETE command takes the general form

*start-line, end-line*D

Start-line and *end-line* are line numbers. The DELETE command will delete all lines from *start-line* to *end-line*. For example, using the EDTEST.TXT file, try this command

3,5D

and then list the file. Your screen will look like this.

```
1: This is before line one
2: this is new line two
3:*Text editors
4: are fun to use
5: as long as you know the
6: right commands.
```

If you do not specify the starting line number, the DELETE command will delete all lines from the current line to the ending line. However, you must start this form of the command with the comma. For example, this command would delete lines 3 and 4 in this example because the current line is line 3 and you would be telling EDLIN to delete from current line to line 4.

```
,4D
```

You could delete any one line by simply specifying its line number. For example, this would delete line 2.

```
2D
```

Notice that no comma precedes this form of the command.

Finally, if no line number is specified, the current line is deleted.

LISTING THE FILE

So far you have seen only the simplest form of the L command. Its general form is

*start-line, end-line*L

where *start-line* and *end-line* specify a range of lines to list on the screen. For example, to list the lines 3 through 5, enter

```
3,5L
```

This will display

```
3:*Text editors
4: are fun to use
5: as long as you know the
```

If you omit the starting line number, EDLIN will display 11 lines before the current line and stop at the specified ending line. You must start this form of the command with a comma.

Omitting the ending line causes EDLIN to display 23 lines beginning with the specified line. If fewer than 23 lines remain, EDLIN will display lines until the end is reached. For example, still using EDTEST.TXT, the command

```
4L
```

causes the following display:

```
4:    are fun to use
5:    as long as you know the
6:    right commands.
```

If no line numbers are specified, then 11 lines before and after the current line are displayed. This makes a total of 23 lines (if there are that many in the file).

EDITING LINES

You can edit (modify) an existing line in a file by first entering its line number. The specified line will be displayed and the cursor positioned beneath the first character in the line. You can use any of the DOS editing keys to make changes to the line. The process of editing an existing line is called *intraline editing*.

For example, enter 2 now. You will see the following:

```
2:*this is new line two
2: _
```

You may now edit this line exactly as you would the DOS command line.

For example, press F1 until the cursor is positioned past the space following the word *is*. Now press I, enter **a new addition to**, and then press F3 followed by ENTER. When you list the file, line 2 will look like this:

```
2:*this is a new addition to new line two
```

Once you press ENTER, any changes you have made to the line will be part of the file. You can cancel the edit at any time by pressing either ESC or CTRL-BREAK. If you have not moved the cursor from the start of the line, then pressing ENTER will also cancel the intraline editing process.

You may edit the current line by entering a period instead of its line number.

Try some examples of intraline editing now.

COPYING LINES

The C (COPY) command is used to copy a range of lines. It has the general form

*start-line, end-line, dest-line, count*C

The lines between *start-line* and *end-line*, inclusive, are copied before *dest-line count* number of times. If *count* is not specified, the default is one.

For example, once again using the EDTEST.TXT file, enter the following command:

```
1,3,6C
```

The file will now look like this.

```
1: This is before line one
2: this is new line two
3:*Text editors
4: are fun to use
5: as long as you know the
```

```
6: This is before line one
7: this is new line two
8: Text editors
9: right commands.
```

Remember that a copy duplicates lines, which means that the lines copied are still in their original place as well as in the new location. The MOVE command (discussed next) is used to move lines from one spot to another.

If you specify a count value, the specified lines will be duplicated that many times. For example, try the following command:

```
1,1,4,3C
```

Your file will now look like this.

```
 1: This is before line one
 2: this is new line two
 3: Text editors
 4:*This is before line one
 5: This is before line one
 6: This is before line one
 7: are fun to use
 8: as long as you know the
 9: This is before line one
10: this is new line two
11: Text editors
12: right commands.
```

Keep in mind that the destination line must be outside the range of the lines to be copied.

MOVING LINES

The M (MOVE LINES) command is similar to the COPY command except that it moves the specified range of lines from one spot in the file to another. Its general form is

*start-line, end-line, dest-line*M

Before proceeding, let's clean up the EDTEST.TXT file. First delete all existing lines by entering **1,100D**. Then insert the following lines:

```
one
two
three
four
five
six
seven
eight
nine
ten
```

Once you have done this, try the following command:

```
2,5,8M
```

List the file; it will look like this.

```
 1: one
 2: six
 3: seven
 4:*two
 5: three
 6: four
 7: five
 8: eight
 9: nine
10: ten
```

As you can see, the original lines 2 through 5 have been relocated to the position immediately before line 8.

If you leave off either (or both) the starting or ending line, the current line is used by default. For example, executing this command would move line 4 to the top of the file.

```
,,1M
```

As with the COPY command, the destination must not be within the range to be moved.

SEARCHING

To find a specific string in the file, use the S (SEARCH) command. A *string* is simply a sequence of characters. The SEARCH command takes the general form

```
start-line, end-line, ? Sstring
```

This command searches the file between *start-line* and *end-line* looking for an occurrence of *string*. The question mark (?) is optional and is used to find multiple occurrences.

To begin, delete all the lines in the file and enter the following:

This is a test
of the search command.
From time to time,
you will find this command useful—
especially when the file is very large.

Once you have entered these lines, try the following command:

```
1,5Stime
```

EDLIN will display

```
3: From time to time,
```

The line in which a match is found is also made current.

If you want to search for a specific occurrence of a string that appears more than once in the file, use the question mark (?) option. For example, enter the following command:

```
1,5?Sthe
```

You will first see

```
        2: of the search command.
O.K.? _
```

As you can see, the question mark causes EDLIN to ask you whether the proper occurrence of the string has been found. If it has, press Y or ENTER; otherwise, press any other key. Press N at this time. EDLIN will find the second "the" in line 5 and will once again prompt you. Press N again. Because "the" does not occur again in the file, EDLIN prints the message "Not found."

The SEARCH command is case sensitive, which means that upper- and lowercase versions of the same character are considered to be different. For example, try

```
1,5?SThis
```

EDLIN finds the match with "This" in the first line but does not report any other matches because the "this" in line 4 begins with a lowercase "t."

If you omit the first line number, the SEARCH command begins with the line immediately following the current line. Omitting the second line number causes the search to continue until the last line in the file. If you omit the search string, the previous string is used.

Try some examples of searching at this time.

REPLACING TEXT

To replace one string with another, you use the R (REPLACE) command. The general form of the REPLACE command is

start-line, end-line ?R*old-string*<F6>*new-string*

The first two line numbers define the range over which the replacement will take place. The question mark (?) is optional. If used, you are prompted prior to each replacement. The old string is the one to be replaced by the new string. You separate the old and new strings by pressing the F6 key.

Using the file developed in the section on searching, try the following command:

```
1,5Rtime<F6>day
```

Note that the F6 key displays as a CONTROL-Z. This command will change line 3 from

From time to time

to

From day to day

If you do not want to change all occurrences of a string, use the question mark (?) option. You will be prompted at each occurrence whether you want to change it or not. For example, to change the sentences to past tense, use the following command:

```
1,5?Ris<F6>was
```

The first thing you see is

```
        1: Thwas is a test
O.K.? _
```

As you can see, EDLIN found the "is" in "This." Because you do not want to change this "is" to "was," press N — EDLIN will then look for other occurrences. The next one is the one that you want to change.

```
        1: This was a test
O.K.? _
```

Because you want to change this "is," press Y. This process will continue until the full five lines have been searched.

You can use the REPLACE command to remove unwanted text by leaving the new string blank. For example, try the following command:

```
1,5Ra<F6>
```

As you can see, all the "a"s have been removed from the file. The F6 is technically unnecessary in this case.

As with the SEARCH command, omitting the first line number causes the replacements to begin with the line immediately following the current line. If the ending line number is not present, the replacement process ends with the last line in the file. If no strings are specified, the strings from the previous R command are used.

Try some examples at this time.

THE PAGE COMMAND

The P (PAGE) command is used to list a block of lines on the display. It differs from the LIST command in that it resets the current line to be that of the last line displayed. In its simplest form it pages through a file 23 lines at a time. This is done by simply entering "P" repeatedly. Its general form is

```
start-line, end-line P
```

If present, *start-line* and *end-line* specify a range of lines to display. If *start-line* is omitted, the line following the current line is used. If *end-line* is not specified, then 23 lines are listed.

END EDIT AND QUIT

The E (END EDIT) command terminates the editing process and saves the file as described earlier. The Q (QUIT) command terminates the editor but does not save what has been edited.

TRANSFERRING TEXT BETWEEN FILES

EDLIN allows you to read the contents of a file on disk into the file you are currently editing by using the T (TRANSFER) command. So that you can follow along, create two files called TEST1.TXT and TEST2.TXT with EDLIN. Enter these lines into TEST1.TXT.

```
one
two
three
four
```

Into TEST2.TXT, enter

This is a test

Now edit TEST1. Try the following command:

```
3TTEST2.TXT
```

Now list the file. It will look like this.

```
one
two
This is a test
three
four
```

As you can see, the contents of TEST2 were read into TEST1 immediately before line 3.

The TRANSFER command takes the general form

*line-num*T*filename*

where *line-num* is the number of the line before which the text from the disk file will be placed. The *filename* is the name of the file to read in. If no line number is specified, the text is placed before the current line.

There are three things to remember about the TRANSFER command. First, the text is read in immediately before the line specified. Second, if the file is not in the current directory, you will receive the message "File not found." Finally, the entire contents of the disk file are read in; it is not possible to read in just part of a file.

APPEND AND WRITE

When you are editing a file that is too large to fit in memory, EDLIN reads in the file until 75 percent of free memory is used. You can tell EDLIN to read in more lines by using the A (APPEND) command. The APPEND command has the general form

*num-lines*A

where *num-lines* is the number of lines to read in. If no number is specified, then one line is read. For example, 45A reads in 45 more lines.

To edit the end of a large file, you must write part of it out to disk in order to free memory before issuing the APPEND command. To do this, you use the W (WRITE) command, which has the general form

*num-lines*W

Num-lines refers to the number of lines to write to the disk. If a number is not specified, text is written until 75 percent of memory is free. The WRITE command writes lines from the top of the file starting with line 1.

SUMMARY

In this chapter you learned to use EDLIN, including how to

- Insert, edit, and delete text
- List the file
- Move and copy text
- Search for and replace character sequences
- Read the contents of one file into another

In the next chapter you will learn how to create your own DOS commands.

8

BATCH FILES

You will sometimes want to give the computer a list of commands all at once and then have the computer whir away on its own without further interaction from you until the list of commands has been executed. For example, you might want to tell the computer to prepare payroll information, print checks, and create weekly backup files without having to wait for each task to be completed before giving the next command. The creation of lists of commands is the subject of this chapter.

In this chapter we assume that you have your DOS work disk in drive A or are using a fixed disk.

WHAT ARE BATCH FILES?

DOS allows you to create lists of commands through the use of *batch files*. A batch file is simply a text file that contains one or more DOS commands. All batch file names must have the extension .BAT. Once you have created a batch file, you cause DOS to execute the commands in the file by entering the name of the batch file at the DOS prompt as if it were a DOS external command. In fact you can think of batch files as custom commands that you create.

TWO SIMPLE BATCH FILES

As an easy first example, use EDLIN (or another text editor) to create a file called TEST.BAT that contains the following lines:

```
DIR
CHKDSK
```

Now enter TEST at the command line. As you can see, DOS first lists the directory and then executes CHKDSK. (Note that you do not use the extension when you enter a batch file's name at the prompt.)

How It Works

When you enter a command at the DOS prompt, a sequence of events begins. First, DOS checks to see if the string of characters that you entered matches one of DOS's internal commands. If it does, then that command is executed. Otherwise, DOS checks the current disk to see if what you entered at the prompt matches one of DOS's external commands or an application program. (Remember, all DOS external commands and programs end with the .EXE or .COM extension.) If the command or program is found, it is executed. Otherwise, DOS checks to see if there is a batch file that matches what you entered at the DOS prompt. If one exists, DOS sequentially executes the commands in the batch file, starting with the first and finishing with the last.

Batch file commands must not have the same name as any other DOS command or application program that you are using. If you accidentally create a batch file with the same name as a DOS command, DOS will always execute the command—never the batch file.

A Second Example

You will find that you often execute the same sequence of commands over and over again. For example, if you are using an accounting program, then you may make copies of all the data files at the end of each day. Assume that the data files are called REC.DAT, EMP.DAT, INV.UPD,

WITHHOLD.TAX, and PAYABLE.DAT. To copy these files from drive C to A, you would enter the following commands:

```
COPY *.DAT A:
COPY INV.UPD A:
COPY WITHHOLD.TAX A:
```

However, had you created a batch file that contains these commands and called it BKUP.BAT, then you could just enter BKUP to copy the files.

To see how such a command will work, use EDLIN to create three files called SAMPLE1.TXT, SAMPLE2.TXT, and SAMPLE3.TXT. Enter a few characters of your own choosing into each. Now create the BKUP.BAT file that contains the following commands:

```
COPY SAMPLE1.TXT A:
COPY SAMPLE2.TXT A:
COPY SAMPLE3.TXT A:
```

(If you have two floppies, use B as the destination drive.) Place a diskette into drive A (or B for two-floppy systems) and enter BKUP at the prompt. You will see DOS copy the files.

Although creating a batch file command certainly saves some typing, the command's main advantage is its reliability. Once you have created a batch command, it will always do exactly what you want it to do. You needn't worry about it accidentally forgetting to copy a file, for example.

CANCELING A BATCH COMMAND

The easiest way to cancel a batch command once it begins is to press the CTRL-BREAK key. (The CTRL-C key sequence also works.) Depending upon what commands make up the batch command, DOS may wait until the current command finishes before stopping the batch command. DOS will prompt you with the following message:

```
Terminate batch job (Y/N)? _
```

If you really want to stop execution of the batch command, press Y;

otherwise, press N and the command will continue to run. If any of the commands that make up the batch file have already been executed by DOS, their effects will not be nullified. For example, if the first command erases some file, subsequently stopping the batch command will not prevent the file from being erased.

ADDING PARAMETERS

You will often want to create a batch command that will operate slightly differently depending upon how it is used. For example, consider these two batch files.

```
batch file  1                    batch file  2

COPY SAMPLE1.TXT A:              COPY SAMPLE2.TXT A:
COMP SAMPLE1.TXT A:              COMP SAMPLE2.TXT A:
```

As you can see, the only difference between file 1 and file 2 is the file name used in the COPY and COMP commands. In this section you will learn how to create one batch file that can replace these two batch files by using placeholders instead of actual file names.

Replaceable Parameters

DOS allows you to use up to 10 *replaceable parameters* (sometimes called *dummy parameters*) as placeholders in a batch file. These replaceable parameters are called %0 through %9. Each piece of information that you pass to the batch file is called an *argument* and is placed on the command line immediately after the batch file name. For this reason, these are called *command line arguments*. Each replaceable parameter in a batch file is replaced by its corresponding argument. Parameter %0 will be replaced by the name of the batch file if you are using 3.2 or newer versions of DOS. Parameter %1 will contain the first argument on the command line, %2 will contain the second argument, and so on. For example, create a batch file called CPYFILE.BAT that contains the following line:

```
COPY %1 %2
```

When you enter this line at the DOS prompt,

```
CPYFILE SAMPLE1.TXT TEMP
```

parameter %1 will contain SAMPLE1.TXT and %2 will have the value TEMP. (In this and the rest of the examples in this book, the %0 parameter is not needed and is not used.) Try this now.

The most important thing to remember about the command line arguments used in a batch command is that they must be separated by spaces. DOS does not recognize any other character as a separator. Thus, the string

```
this,is,a,test
```

will be seen by DOS as one argument, not four. Also, because the space is used as a separator, you cannot use an argument that contains spaces. Thus, this line will be seen as four separate arguments by DOS.

```
this is a test
```

A Practical Example of Parameterized Batch Files

As you remember from Chapter 7, each time you reedit a file using EDLIN, a backup copy is created that contains the previous version of the file. Assume for the moment that the disk you are using is nearly full and does not have enough room for backup copies of the files. This means that each time you finish editing a file, you will also want to erase its backup. You could manually erase the file, but a better way is to create a batch file command that automatically erases the backup when you are done editing.

To see how to accomplish this, create a file called ED.BAT and put the following commands in it:

```
EDLIN %1.%2
ERASE %1.BAK
```

Each time you want to edit a file, use the ED batch command like this.

ED *filename extension*

If the file that you wish to edit does not have an extension, do not specify one—DOS will then leave %2 blank. After the editing session ends, the ERASE command will be executed, removing the backup file from the disk. You might want to try this batch command now.

SPECIAL BATCH FILE COMMANDS

DOS allows you to use some special batch file commands that give you greater control over how a batch file is interpreted or operates. These special commands let you create batch files that are actually a little like programs. We will discuss these commands now.

The ECHO Command

The ECHO command has two uses. First, it is used to control whether DOS displays the commands in a batch file. By default, ECHO is on, which means that DOS displays each command in the batch file as it is executed. If ECHO is turned off, the batch commands will not be displayed, but any output produced by the commands will still be shown. The second use of the ECHO command is to print messages to the screen.

The ECHO batch command takes the general form

ECHO *on*/*off*/*message*

To turn ECHO off, enter

```
ECHO OFF
```

To turn it on, enter

```
ECHO ON
```

For example, create a file called E.BAT and enter these lines into it:

```
ECHO OFF
VER
```

When you execute this batch file (by pressing E at the prompt), you will see the output of the VER command, but you will not see DOS actually execute the command. The output displayed by this batch file looks like this:

```
C>ECHO OFF

IBM Personal Computer DOS 3.30
C>
```

For comparison, remove the ECHO command and try the batch command again. This time each command is displayed as it is executed. The output now looks like this:

```
C>VER

IBM Personal Computer DOS 3.30
```

As you can see, this time the C>VER was displayed.

To summarize, when ECHO is off, only the output of the commands is displayed on the screen. When ECHO is on, DOS also displays itself executing each command.

When a batch file command sequence concludes, ECHO is automatically turned on.

You can also use ECHO to display a message on the screen. To do this, simply place the message after the ECHO command. For example, the following batch file tells the user what to do if errors are found in a file comparison operation.

```
ECHO OFF
COMP %1 %2
ECHO If errors have been reported, call the office manager.
```

Remember, the message will be displayed whether ECHO is on or off.

Suppressing ECHO One
Line at a Time

If you wish to suppress the display of only certain batch commands, it may be easier to accomplish this on a line-by-line basis. To prevent a batch command from displaying, many versions of DOS allow you to simply place @ in front of the command. For example, DOS will echo all commands except the second one in this batch file.

```
DIR
@COPY %1 %2
CHKDSK
COMP %1 %2
```

The PAUSE Command

You can temporarily stop a batch command by using the PAUSE command, which takes the general form

PAUSE *message*

The *message* is optional. When a PAUSE is encountered, DOS displays the message (if present) and then displays its own message, which is

```
Strike a key when ready . . .
```

DOS will now wait until any key is pressed on the keyboard. You can cancel the batch command by pressing CTRL-BREAK.

The PAUSE command is very useful when a precondition must be met before processing can continue. For example, the following batch file can be used to copy the files on the disk in drive A to the one in drive B. It first prompts you to place the proper diskettes in the drives.

```
PAUSE Put source diskette in A and destination diskette in B
COPY A:*.* B:
```

Your screen will look like this:

```
PAUSE Put source diskette in A and destination diskette in B
Strike a key when ready . . . _
```

Adding Remarks

Sometimes you may want to embed messages and/or notes to yourself (or others) in the batch file to help you remember precisely what the file does. You can do this with the REM command, which has the general form

REM *remark*

The *remark* can be any string from 0 to 123 characters in length. No matter what the remark contains, it will be completely ignored by DOS.

The following batch file command uses remarks to show who created the file and what it is used for.

```
REM Purpose: weekly accounting back-up batch file
REM Author: Herbert Schildt
REM Date of creation: 6/11/87
COPY *.DAT B:
COPY *.INV B:
COPY *.BAK B:
```

It is a good idea to identify your more important batch file commands, as shown in this example, especially when several people will be sharing the same system.

As you begin to write larger batch file command sequences, you will find that remarks help you remember the what and why behind them. Sometimes it is useful to use remarks to give a "play-by-play" description of what a batch file is doing.

The IF Command

It is often useful to create a batch command that does different things depending upon certain conditions. To accomplish this, DOS supports the IF batch file command, which takes the general form

IF *condition command*

Here, *condition* is one of three possible types of conditions and *command* is any other DOS command. If the condition evaluates to TRUE, the command following the condition is carried out. Otherwise, DOS skips the rest of the line and moves on to the next line (if there is one) in the batch file.

DOS allows the IF command to use three different types of conditional expressions. First, you can test two strings for equality. Second, you can check to see if a file exists. Finally, you can see if the previously executed program (or command) terminated because of an error. We will look at examples of these now.

CHECK STRINGS FOR EQUALITY   In DOS a *string* is simply a sequence of characters. You can use the IF to check two strings for equality by using the general form

IF *string1* == *string2 command*

If *string1* equals *string2,* the condition is TRUE; otherwise, it is false. To see a simple example, create a file called CHKSTR.BAT that contains the following lines:

```
ECHO OFF
IF RED == YELLOW ECHO This will not be printed.
IF RED == RED ECHO This you will see.
```

Try this batch command now. As you can see, only the second ECHO statement is executed.

Of course, comparing two strings as shown in the previous example is of little practical value. However, you can use this feature to compare command line arguments. For example, change the CHKSTR.BAT file like this:

```
ECHO OFF
IF %1 == YELLOW ECHO The color is yellow.
IF %1 == RED ECHO The color is red.
```

Now try executing CHKSTR with an argument of RED. As you can probably guess, it reports that the color is red.

For a more useful example, imagine that a computer in a small office is used by George, Fred, and Mary. Assume further that Mary does word processing, George is in charge of accounting, and Fred uses a spreadsheet. You could write one backup batch file command that will back up the files in the proper directory given the name of the person. This batch command might look like this:

```
ECHO OFF
IF %1 == MARY COPY \WP\*.* A:
IF %1 == FRED COPY \SPSHEET\*.* A:
IF %1 == GEORGE COPY \ACC\*.* A:
```

Assuming that this file is called BK.BAT, then to back up her files, Mary need only place a diskette into drive A and enter

```
BK MARY
```

CHECKING FOR A FILE   You can check to see if a file or set of files exists by using the EXIST condition of the IF, which takes the general form

>   IF EXIST *file-name command*

where *file-name* is the name of the file that you are checking for. The *file-name* may include both a drive specifier and a path name. You may also use the question mark (?) and asterisk (∗) wildcards if you wish.

For example, enter the following lines into a file called EXTEST.BAT.

```
ECHO OFF
IF EXIST replaceable.FIL ECHO This should not be found.
IF EXIST SORT.EXE ECHO SORT.EXE is on the disk.
```

Run this now. As you can see, only the message "SORT.EXE is on the disk" is displayed.

You can also use the EXIST condition to provide a double check when copying files. If the file already exists on the destination diskette, the batch file will allow the user to cancel the command if the file should not be overwritten.

```
IF EXIST B:%1 PAUSE B:%1 exists - press control-Break to
cancel COPY %1 B:
```

CHECKING FOR ERRORS   An application program can set an internal DOS variable that indicates whether the program terminated normally or because of an error. For the sake of discussion, call this variable the *error variable*. If a program terminates normally, it sets the error variable to 0, indicating that everything went all right. If it terminates because of an error, it sets the error variable to a number greater than zero. If a program does not actually set the value of the error variable, it is zero by default. DOS lets you check this variable through the use of the ERRORLEVEL condition in the IF command, which takes the general form

IF ERRORLEVEL *n command*

where *n* is a number greater than or equal to zero and represents the error number set by the application program. If the value of the error variable is equal to or greater than *n,* the condition is TRUE.

Frankly, the use of ERRORLEVEL is somewhat complicated, and the command is used most frequently by programmers. However, all programs will set ERRORLEVEL to zero if they terminate normally. Therefore you can use the following form of the IF command in any batch file you create to check for normal program termination before proceeding. (Keep in mind that not all application programs will set this variable when they terminate because of an error, so some errors could be missed.)

```
REM Check to see that the previous program terminated
REM normally.
IF ERRORLEVEL 1 PAUSE Abnormal program termination.
```

Using the NOT

You can precede the IF condition with the word NOT, which will then reverse the outcome of the condition. For example, if

```
EXIST TEST.DAT
```

is TRUE, then

```
NOT EXIST TEST.DAT
```

is FALSE.

To understand how the NOT works, assume that you have an application program that requires the file INFO.DAT to be present on the current disk. You could use the following batch command to check for the file before the program is run.

```
IF NOT EXIST INFO.DAT PAUSE Insert the program disk.
```

Using the GOTO

The GOTO batch command is used to direct DOS to execute the commands in a batch file in a nonsequential order. The general form of the GOTO is

GOTO *label*

where *label* is a label defined elsewhere in the batch file. When the GOTO is executed, DOS goes to the specified label and begins executing commands from that point. Using the GOTO, you can cause execution to jump forward or backward in the file.

For example, create a file called GOTOTEST.BAT and enter the following lines:

```
ECHO OFF
IF %1 == RED GOTO RED
IF %1 == BLUE GOTO BLUE
:RED
ECHO You chose the color red.
DIR
GOTO DONE
:BLUE
ECHO You like blue.
CHKDSK
:DONE
REM The batch file is now finished.
```

Try this batch command with the arguments of BLUE and RED now.

As you can see from the previous example, all labels must begin with a colon. Though a label may be up to 125 characters long, DOS will use only the first 8 because, in the language of computers, only those characters are significant. This means that the following labels will appear the same to DOS.

```
:longlabel1
:longlabel2
```

You may not use a period in a label name.

As the example illustrated, you can use the GOTO in conjunction with the IF to create *blocks of commands* that will be executed only if the condition controlling the IF is TRUE. Notice that you must provide a GOTO around other blocks of commands, as is done with the GOTO DONE in the RED block, if you don't want execution to "fall through" into the next block.

You can use the GOTO and the label to create a loop. For example, the following batch file continues to list the directory until you press CTRL-BREAK, which cancels the command.

```
:ONE
DIR
GOTO ONE
```

The CALL Command

Sometimes you will want to execute another batch file command from within a batch file. The best way to do this is with the CALL command, the general form of which is

CALL *batch-file*

where *batch-file* is the name of the batch file command that you wish to execute.

As a first simple example, create a file called ONE.BAT that contains the following lines:

```
ECHO OFF
ECHO This is in batch file ONE
CALL TWO
ECHO This is back in batch file ONE
```

Now create the file TWO.BAT, which contains the following line:

```
ECHO This is in batch file TWO
```

Now execute batch file ONE. After it has run, your display will look like this:

```
This is in batch file ONE
This is in batch file TWO
This is back in batch file ONE
```

A batch file can call itself, but you must make certain that some terminating condition eventually stops the process.

A good use for CALL is to allow the creation of *master batch files* that simply consist of CALLs to other batch files. Such a master file looks somewhat like an outline and provides a quick way for you to see what is actually happening. (As you create your own batch files, you will be surprised at how long and complicated they can become.) For example, a master batch file for word processing might look like this:

```
REM First create the document
CALL WORDPROC
REM Next, check it for spelling
CALL SPELL
REM Now, print it
CALL PRNT
```

One final point about calling other batch file commands: canceling a CALLed command cancels all batch files, including both the one currently executing and the one that CALLed it.

Repeating Commands with FOR

You can repeat a series of commands using different arguments through the use of the FOR command, which takes the general form

FOR %%*var* IN (*argument list*) DO *command*

where *var* is a single-letter variable that will take on the values of the arguments. The arguments must be separated by spaces. The FOR will repeat the *command* as many times as there are arguments. Each time the FOR repeats, *var* will be replaced by an argument moving from left to right.

For a first simple example, create a file called SIMPFOR.BAT that contains the following commands:

```
ECHO OFF
FOR %%I IN (%1 %2 %3) DO ECHO %%I
```

This batch file will print the first three command line arguments it is called with. For example, execute it with the arguments ONE TWO THREE. The output produced by the FOR will look like this:

```
ONE
TWO
THREE
```

As a second example, create a file called FORTEST.BAT that contains the following commands:

```
ECHO OFF
FOR %%H IN (FORTEST.BAT ONE.BAT TWO.BAT) DO DIR %%H
```

Run FORTEST now. As you can see, the DIR command is executed three times, each time with a different file name. Each time the FOR repeats, %%H is replaced by the next argument in the list. That is, the first %%H equals FORTEST.BAT, the second %%H equals ONE.BAT, and so on. The FOR continues to repeat until the last argument is used.

You can use the FOR to execute a list of commands by placing the commands in the argument list. For example, the following command will first clear the screen, then list the directory, and finally check the disk.

```
FOR %%C IN (CLS DIR CHKDSK) DO %%C
```

You may not use a FOR command as the object of the DO. That is, FOR cannot be used to execute another FOR command.

Using SHIFT

As you know, there are only 10 replaceable parameters, %0 through %9. You can use the SHIFT command to gain access to command line arguments greater than 10. Each time SHIFT is executed, the contents of the replaceable parameters are shifted down one position with whatever was in %0 being lost and %9 containing a new argument if one exists. For example, given these beginning values,

Replaceable Parameter	Value
%0	TEST
%1	A
%2	B
%3	C
%4	<empty>

after one SHIFT, they will have the following values:

Replaceable Parameter	Value
%0	A
%1	B
%2	C
%3	<empty>

As a simple first example, create a file called SHFT.BAT that contains the following commands:

```
ECHO OFF
ECHO %0 %1 %2 %3
SHIFT
ECHO %0 %1 %2 %3
```

Execute the following command as shown here:

```
SHFT ONE TWO THREE
```

You will see this output:

```
SHFT ONE TWO THREE
ONE TWO THREE
```

You can use a loop to make accessing a large number of arguments easier. For example, change the SHFT.BAT file so that it contains the following commands:

```
ECHO OFF
:LOOP
ECHO %1
SHIFT
IF NOT %1 == END GOTO LOOP
REM This will loop until an argument containing
REM the word END is reached.
```

Now execute this batch file as shown here:

```
SHFT THIS IS A TEST THAT ACCESSES EACH ARGUMENT END
```

This will display the following:

```
THIS
IS
A
TEST
THAT
ACCESSES
EACH
ARGUMENT
```

EXECUTING A BATCH FILE FROM WITHIN A BATCH FILE

You can start another batch file command from within a batch file without using the CALL command. However, executing a batch file command without using CALL produces different results than when the CALL is used. To cause one batch file to execute another, simply use the name of the batch file like any other command. When the batch file's name is encountered, DOS will automatically stop executing the first batch file and begin executing the second. However, when that file terminates, control returns to DOS and the prompt is displayed — DOS does not return to the original batch file.

For example, assume that BKUP is the name of a batch file. Then, given the following batch file:

```
CLS
CHKDSK
BKUP
DISKCOMP A: B:
```

the final line will never be executed. If you want control to return to the original batch file, use the CALL command.

AUTOEXEC.BAT

There is one very special batch file, AUTOEXEC.BAT, that you will probably want to create. This is the batch file that DOS automatically executes at startup. (If AUTOEXEC.BAT is not on the DOS disk, then the DATE and TIME commands are executed by DOS instead.) You will often want DOS to perform one or more tasks when the computer is first started. Place these tasks in the AUTOEXEC.BAT file.

A very simple AUTOEXEC.BAT file might look like this:

```
DATE
TIME
CLS
```

Because the AUTOEXEC.BAT file exists, DOS no longer automatically executes the DATE and TIME commands; you must include them in the file. After they are executed, DOS clears the screen. Create this file now and restart your computer to see how it works.

You can use the AUTOEXEC.BAT file to create a "custom look" to your system. For example, a computer dedicated to word processing might use the following AUTOEXEC.BAT file:

```
DATE
TIME
CLS
ECHO WELCOME TO WORD PROCESSING
ECHO           AT WIDGET CORP.
PAUSE
CD \WP
```

You can also use the AUTOEXEC.BAT file to confirm that the proper programs are available for use. For example, assume that the program ACCOUNT.EXE is required for the operation of the computer and that it must be located on drive A. The following AUTOEXEC.BAT file will wait until you put a diskette containing ACCOUNT.EXE into drive A.

```
ECHO OFF
DATE
TIME
:LOOP
IF EXIST A:ACCOUNT.EXE GOTO OK
ECHO  Insert program diskette into drive A
PAUSE
GOTO LOOP
:OK
```

Later in this book you will learn that there are several ways to customize DOS, and some of these customization commands are perfect candidates for inclusion in the AUTOEXEC.BAT file.

SUMMARY

In this chapter you learned how to create custom DOS commands through the use of batch files. You learned

- How to parameterize a batch file
- About the special batch commands

      ECHO
      PAUSE
      CALL
      REM
      IF
      FOR
      GOTO
      SHIFT

- About the AUTOEXEC.BAT file and its special purpose in DOS

In the next chapter you will learn some advanced commands that will give you even greater power over your computer.

9

MORE DOS COMMANDS

Now that you know the basics of DOS, it is time for you to learn about some more DOS commands that give you greater control over the computer. Some of these commands are fairly complicated, but they yield great returns for the time you invest.

ATTRIB

DOS associates a set of file attributes with each file on disk. Most of these attributes are for DOS's internal use and cannot be examined or modified. However, you can examine and set the *archive* and *read-only* attributes with the ATTRIB command. ATTRIB is an external command.

The general form of the ATTRIB command is

ATTRIB *attribute file-name*

where *attribute* is either not present or is one of the following:

+R   turn on read-only attribute

−R   turn off read/write attribute

+A   turn on archive attribute

−A   turn off archive attribute

The *file-name* is the name of the file, including drive and path specifiers, that will have its attributes changed.

Before going on, let's discuss what these two attributes do. The archive attribute is used primarily by DOS to streamline the process of backing up the fixed disk. Although we will examine this attribute closer when we discuss fixed-disk backup, the following brief discussion will give you the general idea. Each time a file is created or modified, the archive attribute is turned on. During the backup process, the archive attribute is turned off. During subsequent backups, you can copy only those files that have changed since the last backup because only those that have changed will have the archive attribute on. You usually don't need to change the archive attribute, and it is best left alone.

The read-only attribute is used to determine whether a file can be modified. A file that has the read-only attribute turned on can be read but not written to. That is, it cannot be changed. When the read-only attribute is turned off, the file can be read or written to. Generally, when a file is created, the read-only attribute is turned off. The main reason that you would want to turn on the read-only attribute is to prevent unauthorized or accidental tampering with an important file.

You will need a file to use with the examples, so use EDLIN to create a text file called TEST that contains a few characters of your own choosing. You can examine the attribute setting of TEST with the ATTRIB command by not specifying an attribute. For example, enter the following:

```
ATTRIB TEST
```

DOS will respond with

```
A       C:\TEST
```

The "A" signifies that the archive attribute is turned on, as you would expect because TEST is a new file.

To set a file to read-only mode, use the **+R** argument. For example, enter the following command:

```
ATTRIB +R TEST
```

Now examine the attribute settings again by using ATTRIB without any attribute arguments. You will now see this display:

```
A    R  C:\TEST
```

which tells you that TEST is now in read-only mode.

   To summarize: when an attribute is turned on, its first letter is displayed; when it is turned off, nothing is displayed.

   To see the effect of read-only, first try to reedit the file with EDLIN. It will respond with

```
File is READ-ONLY
```

and will not allow you to edit TEST. Now try to erase TEST. You will see this message:

```
Access denied
```

DOS will not let you erase a read-only file. However, try the following command:

```
TYPE TEST
```

Because TYPEing a file involves only reading it, DOS lets you look at it. You can also use PRINT to print it and COPY to copy it. You simply cannot change it.

   To turn off the read-only attribute, use the following command:

```
ATTRIB -R TEST
```

Now try erasing the file. As is evident, the file is now erased.

   You can use the wildcard characters * and ? in the file name, but you should do so with caution because you will be setting the attributes of all the files specified.

   You can change the attributes of all files in a directory, plus those in any subdirectories, by placing a /S after the end of the file name. (Be sure to leave a space between the file name and the /S.) For example, the following command will set the archive attribute of all files with the .TXT extension on a disk in drive A. DON'T TRY THIS EXAMPLE.

```
ATTRIB +A A:*.TXT /S
```

LABEL AND VOL

When you list the directory of the DOS diskette, the first line looks like this:

```
Volume in Drive A has no label
```

Until now we have been ignoring this message. Here you will learn to give a disk a volume label.

What Is a Volume Label?

A volume label is essentially a name for a disk — either floppy or fixed. It can be up to 11 characters long and may consist of any characters allowed in a file name. Note, however, that a period is not allowed in the volume label.

There are really only two reasons why you should give a disk a volume label. The first is that it helps you to positively identify the disk. This can be useful when you are trying to remember which disk is which. However, the volume label should never take the place of the external stick-on label. The second reason is that in the future, new versions of DOS may allow you to access a disk by its volume name instead of by drive letter.

Using LABEL

Use the external DOS LABEL command to give a disk a name. Place your DOS work disk in drive A and switch to drive A now. (This instruction also applies to fixed-disk users.) To execute LABEL, simply enter LABEL at the DOS prompt. You will see the following:

```
Volume in drive A has no label

Volume label (11 characters, ENTER for none)?_
```

Now enter the label WORKDISK and then try the DIR command.

The first line will now look like this:

```
Volume in drive A is WORKDISK
```

You can change the volume label by simply using LABEL to enter a new name. To remove a volume label, press ENTER instead of specifying a new name. DOS will then prompt you, as shown here.

```
Delete current volume label (Y/N)?
```

At this point you can either remove the volume label or abort the LABEL command.

You can specify the volume label on the command line as an argument to LABEL. For example, the following command changes the volume label to MYDISK.

```
LABEL MYDISK
```

In this form of the command, DOS does not display any messages.

You can place a drive specifier in front of the label in the command line version to change the volume label of a disk other than the current one. For example, the following command sets the volume label of the diskette in drive B to SAMPLE.

```
LABEL B:SAMPLE
```

VOL

To see the volume label, enter the VOL command. For example, enter VOL now and you will see the following:

```
Volume in drive A is WORKDISK
```

You can use a drive specifier with VOL to see the volume label of a disk in a drive other than the current one. For example, the following command displays the volume label for drive B.

```
VOL B:
```

A CLOSER LOOK AT FORMAT

Though you learned the basics of the FORMAT command earlier, you should now become familiar with some of its many options. All FORMAT options use the same form—a division sign followed by the option character. There can be more than one option present.

Specifying a Volume Label

You can specify a volume label for a disk when you format it by using the /V option. For example, the following command lets you add a volume label to the diskette that will be formatted in drive A.

```
FORMAT A: /V
```

After the disk is formatted, you will see this prompt:

```
Volume label (11 characters, ENTER for none)?
```

which is the same prompt used by the LABEL command.

Putting the System Files on a Diskette

For a diskette to be able to load DOS requires that at least three files be present on the disk. These files are

- COMMAND.COM
- IBMBIO.COM
- IBMDOS.COM

On some systems these files may have slightly different names. Collectively, they are called the *DOS system files,* or *system* for short. Loosely, they form different parts of the DOS program. Only COMMAND.COM will show up when the directory is listed; the other two will be hidden. For somewhat technical reasons, IBMBIO.COM and IBMDOS.COM must be the first files on a disk, so, as an option, FORMAT will copy these files onto the newly formatted diskette. The option to specify this is / S. Once the formatting has been completed, in addition to the other messages, the message "System transferred" will be displayed.

FORMAT must have access to the system files in order to transfer them to the new diskette. If they are not on the current disk, you will be prompted to insert a system diskette so that the system files can be copied.

Although a diskette formatted with the / S option can start the computer and load DOS, you will have access only to DOS's internal commands because the external ones are not transferred to the new diskette. However, you can copy the external commands onto the diskette.

Leaving Room for the System Files

DOS is a copyrighted program that you may use but may not give or sell to anyone else except as described in the DOS license agreement. Therefore, you may need to create a diskette that reserves room for the DOS system files but does not actually copy them to the diskette. For example, you might wish to prepare a diskette for a friend that contains several of your files, but you want to make sure that he or she can put a system on it if necessary. (This is done with the SYS command, which we will discuss a little later in this chapter.) If you don't reserve room, the system cannot be put on the diskette.

Use the / B option during formatting to cause storage for the system to be reserved. No additional messages will be displayed, but room will be set aside for the system files.

TRANSFERRING THE SYSTEM WITH SYS

If a diskette has been formatted with the / B option or if no files are on the diskette, you can copy the system files to it by using the SYS command. SYS has the general form

SYS *drive-specifier*

where *drive-specifier* determines the drive that will receive the system files. SYS is an external command.

To see how SYS works, format a fresh diskette using no options whatsoever. For example, if you are formatting the diskette in drive B, enter

```
FORMAT B:
```

Now, if you do not have a fixed disk, make sure that A is the current drive and that your DOS work diskette is in it. Put the blank formatted diskette into B. (If you only have one disk drive, you will need to swap diskettes.) If you have a fixed disk, put the freshly formatted diskette into A and make sure that C is the current drive.

First, let's do a little experiment. Copy the file SORT.EXE to the newly formatted diskette. Now try to put the system files on it by entering

```
SYS B:
```

if you do not have a fixed disk or

```
SYS A:
```

if you do. DOS will respond with this message:

```
No room for system on destination diskette
```

This message is displayed because the system files must occupy the very first sectors and tracks on a diskette. When you copied SORT.EXE to the diskette, it was written to those first sectors and tracks. Thus DOS could not put the system files where they belonged. Had you formatted the diskette with the / B option, however, the first few tracks would have been reserved and the SYS operation would have succeeded.

For SYS to work, you must first erase SORT.EXE from the diskette. Do so now. With the diskette once again blank, try the SYS command again. SYS will respond with the message "System transferred."

There is one little wrinkle in how the SYS command works that you need to know about. As stated previously, there are three system files — IBMDOS.COM, IBMBIO.COM, and COMMAND.COM. For some reason, COMMAND.COM is not transferred by the SYS command. Fortunately, COMMAND.COM can go anywhere on the disk, so its position is not important, but you do need it on any diskette that will be used to start the computer and load DOS. COMMAND.COM is the part

of DOS that interprets your commands. Without it, you cannot communicate with DOS. If you try to use a diskette without COMMAND.COM
to load DOS, you will see this message:

```
Bad or missing Command Interpreter
```

To install COMMAND.COM on the diskette, simply copy it there by
using the COPY command. (It must go in the root directory, however.)

THE VERIFY COMMAND

Disk write operations are usually successful. However, on certain rare
occasions, such as a power surge, an error can occur, and the contents of
the disk file will not be exactly what they are supposed to be. You can
cause DOS to verify that the data has been written correctly. To do this,
DOS actually reads the section of the file just written and compares it to
what is in memory. If a discrepancy is found, a write error is reported.

VERIFY takes the general form

VERIFY *on/off*

By default, VERIFY is off. To turn it on, enter

```
VERIFY ON
```

You might think it a good idea to always have VERIFY turned on, but
it isn't. The reason is that each write operation would take about twice as
long because of the extra work that DOS must do. Turn on VERIFY only
when working with very important files. Remember, disk errors are quite
rare. If you are experiencing frequent errors, your computer should
probably be checked by a qualified service technician.

You can see if VERIFY is on or off by entering VERIFY with no
argument. For example, entering

```
VERIFY
```

now will result in the message

```
VERIFY is on
```

XCOPY: AN EXPANDED COPY COMMAND

Assume that you have a diskette with directories organized like this:

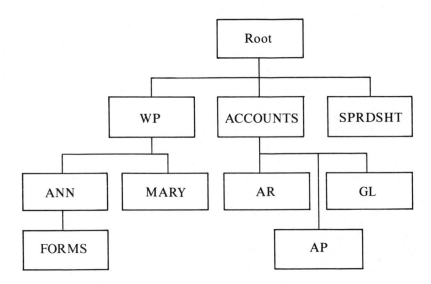

How can you copy the entire contents of the WP directory, including the contents of the ANN and MARY subdirectories plus ANN's subdirectory FORMS, and still maintain the directory structure? With the standard COPY command, you must copy each directory individually, making sure that all files are copied into the correct destination directory. This approach is clearly error prone and tedious. For this reason, DOS versions 3.2 and greater include the XCOPY command, which, in addition to having many other useful features, lets you automatically copy complete sets of directories and subdirectories.

XCOPY is an external command. In its simplest form it works much like COPY. For example, to copy a file called SAMPLE from drive A to drive B, you could use the following command:

```
XCOPY A:SAMPLE B:
```

However, XCOPY goes far beyond this. XCOPY takes the general form

XCOPY *source destination options*

where *source* and *destination* may be a drive specifier, a file name, or a directory name — or any combination of the three. The *options* let you control exactly what and how XCOPY copies.

Let's look at how XCOPY functions with its various options.

Copying Files

Though it is faster to copy files with the internal COPY command, you can copy files using XCOPY. The wildcard characters * and ? are allowed. Also, the /V (verify) option is supported.

Copying Groups of Directories

You can use XCOPY to copy the contents of the current directory plus the contents of any subdirectories. To see how this works, format two diskettes and label them ONE and TWO. On diskette ONE, create these two subdirectories using the following commands. (Fixed-disk users: do *not* use your fixed disk for this example.)

```
MKDIR WP
MKDIR ACCOUNTS
```

Switch to the WP directory and issue the following command:

```
MKDIR LETTERS
```

The directory structure of diskette ONE should now look like this:

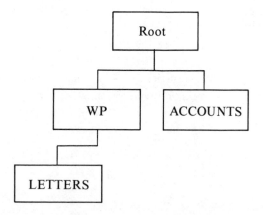

Use EDLIN to create a short text file called SAMPLE.TXT that contains whatever you like in the root directory. Then create another file called SAMPLE2.TXT in the WP directory. Next, create a file called SAMPLE3.TXT in the WP\LETTERS directory. Finally, copy XCOPY.EXE into the root directory of diskette ONE. Put diskette ONE in drive A. If you have a dual-floppy system, put diskette TWO into drive B. Otherwise, you will need to swap it in and out of drive A as prompted by DOS.

As an example, first try the following command:

```
XCOPY A: B:
```

If you only have one floppy drive, DOS will alternately call it A and B, allowing you to swap in the correct diskette. After the command is finished, only the file SAMPLE.TXT from the root directory will have been copied to diskette TWO. You can confirm this by displaying the directory of diskette TWO.

In order for XCOPY to copy the contents of a group of directories, you must use the /S option. Try the following command now:

```
XCOPY A: B: /S
```

After the command has finished, list the directory of diskette TWO. As you can see, the directory WP has been created. If you change to WP, you will see that SAMPLE2.TXT has been copied to that directory and that the subdirectory LETTERS has been created. SAMPLE3.TXT will be found in WP/LETTERS.

The /S option tells XCOPY to copy the contents of the current directory plus all subdirectories. If necessary, it will create the subdirectories on the destination diskette.

You might wonder why the directory ACCOUNTS was not found on diskette TWO. The reason is that ACCOUNTS had no files in it. If a directory contains no entries, XCOPY will not create it on the destination diskette. If you want all directories created, whether empty or not, you must specify the /E option. For example, the following command will cause the ACCOUNTS directory to be created on diskette TWO.

```
XCOPY A: B: /S /E
```

You can copy less than the entire disk by specifying the directory to begin with. For example,

```
XCOPY A:\WP B: /S
```

will copy only the contents of the WP directory plus its subdirectory.

Using the Archive Attribute

You can use XCOPY to copy only files that have the archive attribute turned on by using either the /A or the /M option. Remember that the archive attribute is turned on whenever a file is created or changed. The difference between the two options is what happens to the archive attribute on the source files.

If you use /A, the archive attribute is not changed on the source file, which means that you could make repeated copies of those files with the archive attribute turned on. However, /M causes the archive attribute of the source files to be turned off after they are copied. The reason for this is to allow you an easy way to copy only those files that have changed since the last time a copy was made.

DOS provides a better command, called BACKUP, which also uses the archive attribute to perform backup operations. (You will learn about it a little later on.) It is best to leave this sort of backing up to BACKUP, which is designed expressly for this purpose.

Using the Date Option

You can use XCOPY to copy files based upon their creation dates by using the /D option. This option takes the general form

/D:*mm-dd-yy*

Only those files with creation dates the same as or later than the specified date will be copied. For example,

```
XCOPY A: B: /S /D:12-12-86
```

will copy all files with creation dates beginning with 12-12-86 to the current date of the system.

The / D option applies only to files. Directories will be established on the destination disk without regard to their creation dates.

Query Before Copy

The / P option causes XCOPY to prompt you before each file is copied. The message will take the general form

file-name (Y / N)?

If you press Y, the file is copied. Press N to cause that file to be skipped.

The / W Option

As you have noticed, XCOPY begins to copy files immediately. If you need to switch diskettes before the copying takes place, specify / W, which causes XCOPY to issue the following prompt prior to starting the copying process.

```
Press any key to begin copying file(s)
```

REPLACING FILES

As you continue to use DOS, you will find that there are two very common situations that involve copying files that neither COPY nor XCOPY can handle. The first occurs when you want to replace the files on the destination disk with files of the same name from the source disk. For example, a work disk may contain several files for which a new version exists. The second situation is the opposite of the first. Sometimes you will want to add files to a disk without overwriting any file already on the disk. You can accomplish both of these activities with REPLACE.

The general form of REPLACE is

REPLACE *source destination options*

where *source* and *destination* specify the source and destination file names, directories, or drives, which may include the wildcard characters * and ?.

In its simplest form, REPLACE behaves much like COPY. For example,

```
REPLACE A:SAMPLE B:
```

copies the file SAMPLE from A to B. However, REPLACE really shines when wildcards are used.

Using the two diskettes that you created for the XCOPY examples, create the text file called RPLCTEST.TXT that contains anything you like on disk ONE. Then, copy the file REPLACE.EXE to diskette ONE. Now insert diskette ONE in drive A and B and, if you have two floppies, diskette TWO in drive B. If you only have one floppy, DOS will alternate that drive between A and B and you will be prompted to swap the two diskettes. Now enter

```
REPLACE A:*.* B:
```

Your screen will look like this:

```
A>REPLACE A:*.* B:
  Replacing B:\SAMPLE.TXT
  Replacing B:\XCOPY.EXE
2 File(s) replaced
```

As you can see, REPLACE copied SAMPLE.TXT and XCOPY.EXE but not RPLCTEST.TXT. This is because RPLCTEST.TXT did not exist on the destination disk. Remember, REPLACE will copy only those files that it finds on the destination diskette. In this example only the files in the root directory were replaced. However, if you specify the /S option, then all files in all subdirectories will also be examined and replaced if possible. For example, enter

```
REPLACE A:*.* B: /S
```

As you can see, this replaces all files on the destination diskette in all directories.

You can use REPLACE to add to a disk only those files that are not currently on the destination disk. This prevents existing files from being overwritten. To do this, you use the /A option. Try this command now.

```
REPLACE A:*.* B: /A
```

You will see the following:

```
Adding B:\REPLACE.EXE

Adding B:\RPLCTEST.TXT

2 File(s) added
```

This time the only files copied were those that did not already exist on diskette TWO.

If you need to insert a different diskette before REPLACE begins, use /W, which causes REPLACE to wait until you press a key before beginning.

The /P option causes REPLACE to prompt you before a file is replaced. For example, enter

```
REPLACE A:*.* B: /P
```

You will see the following prompt:

```
Replace B:\SAMPLE.TXT? (Y/N)
```

If you press Y, the file will be replaced; otherwise, it will not.

A couple of points to remember: (1) you cannot use the /A and /S options together, and (2) the source and destination need not be on different disks—they may simply be different directories on the same disk.

PRINTING GRAPHICS IMAGES

When you press the PRTSC key, whatever is on the screen is printed on the printer. However, this will work correctly only for screens that contain text and no graphics. Here, the term *graphics* is used to mean such things as lines, circles, boxes, charts, and the like. Though DOS does not generate graphics displays, many application programs do. To print a screen that contains graphics to the printer, you must first execute the GRAPHICS command. GRAPHICS is an external command.

The GRAPHICS command has the general form

GRAPHICS *printer option*

where the name of *printer* is determined according to the following list:

Printer Type	Name
IBM Personal Graphics Printer	GRAPHICS
IBM Proprinter	GRAPHICS
IBM PC Convertible Printer	THERMAL
IBM Compact Printer	COMPACT
IBM Color Printer with black ribbon	COLOR1
IBM Color Printer with red, green, and blue ribbon	COLOR4
IBM Color Printer with black, cyan, magenta, and yellow ribbon	COLOR8

If no printer name is specified, the IBM Personal Graphics Printer is assumed. The Epson MX-70, MX-80, and MX-100 printers are quite commonly used with microcomputers and are also specified with the GRAPHICS printer name.

For example, to allow graphics to be printed on a color printer with a red, green, and blue ribbon, enter

GRAPHICS COLOR4

By default, white on the screen is printed as black on the printer and black on the screen is printed as white. The /R option causes black to print as black and white to print as white. This option is seldom used.

The background color of the screen is usually not printed. However, if you have a color printer, you can print the background by specifying the /B option.

Finally, the /LCD option should be specified for computers using the IBM PC Convertible Liquid Crystal Display.

SUMMARY

This chapter introduced a number of powerful DOS commands that expand the control you have over the system. These commands are

- ATTRIB
- LABEL
- VOL
- SYS
- VERIFY
- XCOPY
- REPLACE
- GRAPHICS

You also learned how to install the DOS system files on a diskette by using the FORMAT command.

In the next chapter you will learn about filters, pipes, and how to redirect input and output. These elements give you control over how information moves about inside the computer.

10

REDIRECTING I/O

Data goes into the computer via *input* devices and leaves by way of *output* devices. The transfer of information to or from these devices is called an *input/output* operation, or *I/O* operation for short. The computer has several I/O devices, including the keyboard, monitor, printer, and disk drives. By using some special DOS commands, you can reroute the flow of data. This is called *redirected I/O*.

STANDARD INPUT AND STANDARD OUTPUT

You might be surprised to learn that DOS does not "know" where its commands come from or where its output is sent. That is, DOS does not know that you use a keyboard to enter commands and that you see DOS's response on a monitor. This is because DOS does not deal directly with the I/O devices. Rather, it works through two special internal pseudodevices called *standard input* and *standard output*. These pseudodevices provide the programming support for the various I/O devices supported by the computer.

When DOS begins execution, standard input is linked to the keyboard and standard output is linked to the monitor. However, you can

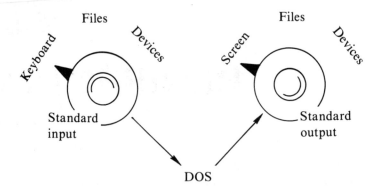

FIGURE 10-1   A depiction of standard input and standard output

change which device is linked with which pseudodevice. For example, you can think of standard input and standard output as depicted in Figure 10-1.

We will look first at the redirection of I/O to and from a disk file. Later you will see how to redirect I/O to the other devices supported by the computer.

For the examples shown in this chapter, make sure that your DOS work disk is in drive A and that A is the current drive, unless you are using a fixed disk, in which case you may use drive C.

REDIRECTING OUTPUT TO A FILE

DOS uses the > and >> operators to redirect the output generated by a DOS command or an application program that would normally be shown on the screen. The general usages of these operators with files are

command > file-name

command >> file-name

where *command* is either a DOS command or an application program

and *file-name* is the name of the file that will receive the output generated
by *command.* For example, enter the following command:

```
DIR > OUT.DIR
```

As you can see, nothing is displayed on the screen.

Now, list the file OUT.DIR on the screen with the TYPE command.
You will see that the output of the DIR command is contained in the file
OUT.DIR. The file OUT.DIR may be edited with EDLIN and is normal
in every way.

The difference between the > and >> operators lies in how the output
file is handled. The > operator always creates a new, empty file to hold the
output information. If a file by the specified name already exists on the
disk, it is first erased and then a new, empty one is created. That is, if
OUT.DIR had already existed on your work disk, the previous example
would have erased it, destroying its contents, and then re-created it and
put the new information into it. However, the >> operator does not
destroy an already existing file. If the specified file already exists, the >>
operator causes the output to be placed on the end of the file. If the file
does not exist, however, it will still be created.

To understand the difference, try the following command:

```
DIR SORT.EXE > OUT.DIR
```

If you now type OUT.DIR, you will see the following output (remember,
the exact information may vary slightly):

```
Volume in drive C is DOSWORK
Directory of C:\

SORT     EXE     1977   3-17-87   12:00P
         1 File(s)   9786787 bytes free
```

As you can see, the old contents of OUT.DIR are no longer present.
However, now try the following command:

```
DIR SORT.EXE >> OUT.DIR
```

Typing OUT.DIR will result in the following display:

```
Volume in drive C is DOSWORK
Directory of C:\
```

```
SORT    EXE    1977   3-17-87  12:00P
        1 File(s)  9786787 bytes free

Volume in drive C is DOSWORK
Directory of C:\

SORT    EXE    1977   3-17-87  12:00P
        1 File(s)  9786787 bytes free
```

As you can see, this time the previous contents of the file were preserved and the new output placed on the end.

You should understand that only the output that would normally go to the screen is being redirected. Other I/O operations performed by the command are not affected. For example, try the following COPY command:

```
COPY OUT.DIR TEST > OUTPUT
```

This command correctly copies the contents of OUT.DIR into TEST. Only the information that COPY sends to standard output will be placed into the file OUTPUT. In this case, OUTPUT will only contain the message "1 File(s) copied."

One of the most common uses of redirected output is to create a *log file* that records the activity of the computer when you are not physically present. For example, the end-of-month phase of an accounting package might include several lengthy operations that are best run overnight. If you place all the commands in a batch file with output redirected into a log file using the $>>$ operator, you can check to see that all went well when you come in the next morning.

REDIRECTING INPUT TO A FILE

You can redirect standard input with the $<$ operator. It has the same basic usage as the $>$ operator. Instead of causing the command to send its output to a file, $<$ causes a command to use the contents of a file as input. When input is redirected, information that is normally entered at the keyboard is read from the specified file.

Though you will seldom need to redirect the input to a command to a file, it is easy enough to do if you are careful. As a simple example, first create a file called INPUT.DAT that contains the word SAMPLE followed by a blank line. Now execute the following command exactly as shown.

```
LABEL < INPUT.DAT
```

Recall that LABEL sets the volume label name of the disk. As you can see, DOS no longer pauses and waits for you to enter the label name. Instead, it reads the name from the file INPUT.DAT. To confirm that this actually happened, use VOL to display the volume label. (You can change the label back to what it was previously, now.)

You must be very careful when redirecting input to a file because, if the file fails to contain sufficient input to satisfy the command, the computer will stop running and lock up. If this happens, the only thing that you can do is restart the system.

A SHORT WARNING

Though all of DOS's commands allow their input and output to be redirected, some application programs do not. Certain programs bypass DOS's standard I/O routines and communicate directly with the hardware — usually to achieve improved performance. In this situation the redirection operators will not be effective. If you attempt to redirect I/O to an application program and it doesn't work right, this is probably the reason.

REDIRECTING I/O TO OTHER DEVICES

You can redirect I/O operations to devices other than disk drives by using their DOS *device names*. These device names and what they refer to are shown in Table 10-1. You cannot create a disk file with the same name as any device name. For traditional reasons, you may place a colon after the device name; however, we will not do so in this book because it is superfluous.

CON	The console, either keyboard or screen
AUX	The first asynchronous serial port
COM1	Same as AUX
COM2	The second asynchronous serial port
COM3	The third asynchronous serial port
COM4	The fourth asynchronous serial port
PRN	The first printer — output only
LPT1	Same as PRN
LPT2	The second printer — output only
LPT3	The third printer — output only
NUL	A nonexistent device used by programmers for testing software

TABLE 10-1   The DOS Device Names

You can use the device names anywhere you would use a file name. For example, create a short text file called **MYNAME** that contains your name. Now try the following command:

```
COPY MYNAME PRN
```

As you can see, your name is printed on the printer, as long as your printer is configured in the standard manner.

Think back to the early chapters in this book, before you knew how to use EDLIN. Now you can understand why you used COPY commands like the one below to create short text files:

```
COPY CON MYFILE
```

This tells COPY to read the keyboard for input. You had to enter a CTRL-Z at the end of the text because CTRL-Z is DOS's end-of-file marker. The COPY command only knows that it is to stop copying reading input when it encounters the end-of-file marker.

As another example, an alternative to using the TYPE command to display the contents of a text file on the screen is to simply COPY it to

CON. For example, the following command prints your name on the screen:

```
COPY MYNAME CON
```

A really slick trick that allows you to use your computer like a very expensive typewriter is the following command:

```
COPY CON PRN
```

Now, whatever you type will be printed on the printer. However, COPY will wait until you enter a CTRL-Z and press ENTER before printing begins.

You can use the I/O redirection operators on device names as well as file names. For example, the following command shows a handy way to print a copy of the directory listing:

```
DIR > PRN
```

Using CTTY

DOS allows you to redirect both the input and output to a different device by using the CTTY (short for Change TeleTYpe) command. The command name is traditional and derives from the early days of computing when teletype machines were used instead of terminals. It is possible to hook up a remote terminal to a DOS-based computer and then switch control of the computer to that terminal. For example, if the terminal were connected to the COM1 serial port, you would enter

```
CTTY COM1
```

to switch control to it. Don't try this, however, unless you know that the device you are switching to can actually control the computer. For example, a printer can't.

To switch control back to the console, enter

```
CTTY CON
```

Unless you have a remote terminal attached to your computer, don't use the CTTY command.

FILTERS

DOS has three special commands that are called *filters* because they read standard input, perform some manipulations on the information, and write it to standard output. The three filter commands are MORE, FIND, and SORT. Let's look at these now.

MORE

The MORE filter command reads standard input, displays 24 lines at a time on the screen, and waits for you to press a key before displaying the next screen full of information. To see how MORE works, create a text file call BIG.TXT that is 50 lines long, with each line containing its line number. That is, the first 10 lines of the file will look like this:

```
1
2
3
4
5
6
7
8
9
10
```

Now try the following command:

```
MORE < BIG.TXT
```

As you can see, the first 24 lines of the file are displayed. On the twenty-fifth line is the prompt

```
-- More --
```

To see more of the file, press any key.

The general form of MORE is

MORE < *file-name/device-name*

Actually, the < and the file or device name are optional. However, if you leave them off, MORE will simply read characters from the keyboard and display them on the screen, which is not very useful.

MORE provides a better way than TYPE does to browse through large text files because it automatically pages through them 24 lines at a time.

FIND

The FIND filter command searches a list of files for occurrences of a specified string and displays each line where a match occurs. FIND has the general form

FIND options *"string" file-list*

The *string* is the sequence of characters that you are looking for and must be enclosed between double quotes. The *file-list* is the list of files that FIND will search. You may not use the wildcard characters in the file names.

Before you can try the examples, you must create a file called SAM-PLE.TXT and enter the following lines into it.

```
This is a sample text
file that illustrates
the use of the FIND filter command.
Notice that upperCASE
and lowercase
are considered separately by FIND.
```

Now try the following command:

```
FIND "that" SAMPLE.TXT
```

FIND will respond with this output:

```
---------- SAMPLE.TXT
file that illustrates
Notice that upperCASE
```

Each time that an occurrence of the search string is found, FIND will respond by printing the line in which the match occurs.

As the contents of the file suggest, FIND treats upper- and lowercase letters separately. For example, try the following command:

```
FIND "CASE" SAMPLE.TXT
```

FIND will only report a match in the line "Notice that upperCASE"; it will not find the lowercase version.

You can specify more than one file to search. To see how this works, copy SAMPLE.TXT to SAMPLE2.TXT and change the first line so that it reads as follows:

```
This is a second sample text
```

Now try the following command:

```
FIND "second" SAMPLE.TXT SAMPLE2.TXT
```

FIND will respond like this:

```
---------- SAMPLE.TXT

---------- SAMPLE2.TXT
This is a second sample text
```

Notice that the files are searched in the order in which they appear on the command line. In this case, the word "sample" occurs only in SAMPLE2.TXT. However, in response to the following command

```
FIND "text" SAMPLE.TXT SAMPLE2.TXT
```

FIND will display

```
---------- SAMPLE.TXT
This is a sample text
```

```
---------- SAMPLE2.TXT
This is a second sample text
```

You may have any number of files in the list, as long as the total length of the command line does not exceed 128 characters.

Sometimes you will only want to know if there are any occurrences of the string and, if so, how many times it appears in the file. To do this, use the /C option. For example, try the following command:

```
FIND /C "that" SAMPLE.TXT
```

FIND will respond like this:

```
---------- SAMPLE.TXT: 2
```

As you can see, only the number of occurrences is reported—the line containing the string is not shown.

You can use the /N option to show the relative line number of each occurrence. Try the following:

```
FIND /N "that" SAMPLE.TXT
```

The output will now look like this:

```
---------- SAMPLE.TXT
[2]file that illustrates
[4]Notice that upperCASE
```

The line numbers are shown between angle brackets. You cannot use the /N and /C options together.

Finally, you can have FIND report all lines that do *not* contain the string by using the /V option. For example, the following command

```
FIND /V "that" SAMPLE.TXT
```

produces this output:

```
This is a sample text
the use of the FIND filter command.
and lowercase
are considered separately by FIND.
```

SORT

The SORT filter command sorts information read from standard input and writes the sorted version to standard output. SORT has the general form

> SORT option *<input >output*

where *input* and *output* are either file or device names. If they are not specified, the screen is used for output and the keyboard for input. It is not uncommon to have SORT display its output on the screen.

SORT works by sorting information on a line-by-line basis. It treats upper- and lowercase as the same character. Unless you specify otherwise, SORT arranges the information in ascending alphabetical order.

As a simple first example, create a file called SORTTEST.TXT and enter the following lines:

```
one
two
three
four
five
six
seven
eight
nine
ten
```

Now try the following command:

```
SORT <SORTTEST.TXT
```

This will cause SORT to display the sorted file on the screen. The output will look like this:

```
eight
five
four
nine
one
seven
six
ten
three
two
```

You can have the sorted information placed in a file by specifying it. For example, the following command places the information in the file TEMP.

```
SORT < SORTTEST.TXT > TEMP
```

You can sort in reverse order by specifying the /R option. The following command displays the SORTTEST.TXT file in reverse alphabetical order.

```
SORT /R <SORTTEST.TXT
```

One good use for SORT is to sort the directory. To do this, first create a file called OUT.DIR that contains the directory listing by using the following command:

```
DIR > OUT.DIR
```

Now try the following command:

```
SORT < OUT.DIR
```

As you can see, a sorted directory is displayed.

Sorting on a Specific Column

Tables of information are very common. Sometimes it is useful to sort a table using information other than that contained in the first column. Unless directed otherwise, SORT begins sorting with the first character of each line. However, you can tell SORT what character to begin sorting on with the $/+ n$ option, where n is the column to begin with.

For example, a hardware store might keep its inventory in a file similar to the one shown here.

```
item     cost  on hand
pliers   10     10
hammers   8      3
nails     1    100
screws    1      0
```

The store manager could use SORT to sort the data based on the on-hand column to provide an easy way to see which items are out of stock or running low by using the following command:

```
SORT /+13 < SORTTEST.TXT
```

The output is as follows:

```
screws   1      0
hammers  8      3
pliers   10     10
nails    1      100
item     cost on hand
```

The number 13 is used because that is the character position that starts the on-hand column. If you try this example, do not use any tabs in the file.

PIPES

You can route the output of one command into the input of another. This process is called *piping* because you can conceptually think of the information flowing from one command to the next through a pipe. To create a pipe between two programs, you use the ¦ operator, which has the general form

command1 ¦ command2

where the output of *command1* is automatically redirected to the input of *command2*. For example, try the following command:

```
DIR ¦ MORE
```

This causes the directory listing to be sent as input to MORE instead of to the screen. MORE then displays the directory 24 lines at a time.

In the previous section you saw one way to produce a sorted directory listing; however, there is an easier way, as the following command illustrates:

```
DIR ¦ SORT ¦ MORE
```

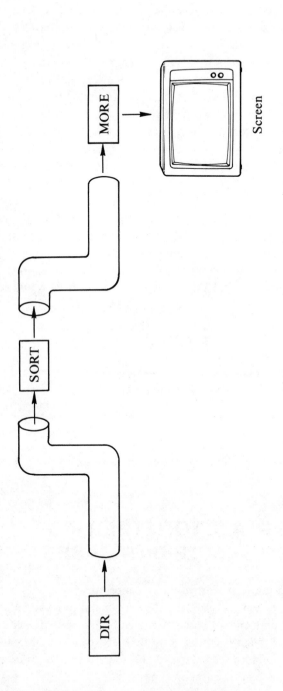

FIGURE 10-2   A visualization of the DIR | SORT | MORE command

Try this. As you can see, the directory is displayed in sorted order. In this case two pipes were used. The output of DIR was used as input by SORT, whose output was in turn used as input by MORE. Figure 10-2 should help you visualize how the following command operates. In general, you can have as many pipes as can fit on the command line.

When a pipe is created, a temporary disk file is established that is automatically erased when the commands are completed. Therefore there must be room on your disk for this temporary file. The size of the file is governed by the amount of output generated by the command that is putting data into the pipe. A few thousand free bytes are usually sufficient.

A very good use for a pipe is to help you find a "lost" file. From time to time, a file will accidentally be placed into the wrong directory of a disk. If there are a great many subdirectories, it can take you a long time to find the file by manually searching each directory. However, the following command will search all directories on a disk and report the path to the file. The file is called TEST here, but in reality you would substitute the name of the file that you are looking for.

```
CHKDSK /V | FIND "TEST"
```

If you remember, when CHKDSK is used with the /V option, it displays all the files on the disk in the basic form

drive:path \file-name

Hence, when a match is reported, the path to the file is shown.

PUTTING IT ALL TOGETHER —
CREATING SIMPLE DATABASES

You can use I/O redirection and pipes to create simple but effective databases. You can use the FIND command to locate information, the SORT command to sort the database, and the MORE command to browse through it. You will use EDLIN (or any other editor) to enter information into the database. The only restriction is that each entry in the database must be on one line.

As a simple example, let's develop a quick-reference telephone directory database of frequently called numbers. The database will use the basic format

Last-name, First-name area-code number

For example:

```
Bell, Alexander 123 555-1010
```

For the sake of the examples, enter the following information into PHONE.DAT:

```
Washington, George 111 555-1111
Bell, Alexander 222 555-2222
Newton, Issac 333 555-3333
Nietzsche, Friedrich 444 555-4444
```

To find Newton's telephone number, you would use the following command:

```
TYPE PHONE.DAT | FIND "Newton"
```

A second or so later, Newton's phone number will appear.

You can sort your phone list using the following series of commands:

```
SORT < PHONE.DAT > TEMP
COPY TEMP PHONE.DAT
ERASE TEMP
```

You can list the numbers for groups of people based on the beginning letters in their names. For example, the following command lists the telephone numbers for both Newton and Nietzsche.

```
TYPE PHONE.DAT | FIND "N"
```

You can expand the telephone directory to include addresses or perhaps remarks, as long as everything fits on one line.

You can use the same basic approach to create databases for other items. The possibilities are limited only by your imagination.

SUMMARY

In this chapter you learned

- About standard input and output
- How to redirect I/O
- About DOS devices
- About the filter commands SORT, FIND, and MORE
- About pipes
- How to create simple databases using DOS

11

CONFIGURING DOS

There are several things about DOS that you can change. Some affect the way DOS operates or appears, while others alter the way DOS accesses disk drives or defines devices. You can also configure DOS for use in a foreign country. In this chapter you will learn the commands that let you configure DOS to best meet your needs.

CHANGING THE DOS PROMPT

By default, the DOS system prompt displays the current drive followed by a > symbol. However, you can change the prompt to display practically anything you want by using the PROMPT command. The general form of the PROMPT command is

PROMPT *message*

where *message* is a string that will become the new system prompt. For example, enter

```
PROMPT My Computer:
```

Now DOS displays the prompt as

```
My Computer:_
```

To return the DOS prompt to its default message, enter PROMPT without a message.

Though short prompts are usually the best, the prompting message can be up to 128 characters long. For example, you might use a prompt like the following to discourage unauthorized use:

```
PROMPT  Warning: authorized users only!
```

You can include special characters and other information in the prompt by using one or more of the codes shown in Table 11-1. All PROMPT codes begin with a dollar sign. Because the characters $>$, $<$, $|$, and $=$ have special meanings when they appear on a DOS command line, you must use the proper code if you want one of these characters to appear in the prompt.

One of the most popular prompts is created with the following command:

```
PROMPT $p$g
```

Code	Meaning
$$	Dollar sign
$b	$|$ character
$d	System time
$e	Escape character
$g	$>$ character
$h	A backspace
$l	$<$ character
$n	Current drive letter
$p	Current directory path
$q	Character
$t	Current time
$v	DOS version number
$_	Carriage return-linefeed sequence

TABLE 11-1   The PROMPT Codes

This causes the current directory path name to be displayed, followed by the > standard DOS prompt. For example, if the current path is C: \ACCOUNTS \AP, the DOS prompt will look like this:

```
C:\ACCOUNTS\AP>
```

This prompt is so popular because it makes it easy to tell what directory you are in. You might want to put this prompt command into the AUTOEXEC.BAT file so that it automatically executes upon startup.

Another popular prompt is formed with the following command:

```
PROMPT $d $t $p$g
```

This causes the current system date and time to be displayed along with the directory path. If the date were 6/19/87, the time 12 noon, and the root directory were current, the prompt would look like this:

```
Fri 6-19-1987 12:00:00.00 C:\>
```

Experiment to see what sort of prompt you like best and then place that PROMPT command into the AUTOEXEC.BAT file.

USING THE MODE COMMAND

As you know, DOS controls the devices that constitute the computer. Some of these devices have various modes of operation. When DOS starts, these devices are set to operate in a way that applies to the widest range of situations. However, you can change the way some of the devices operate to take best advantage of how your system is configured. You can use MODE to change the operation of the video adapter, the serial communication ports, and the printer. Let's look at each area separately.

Controlling the Video Adapter

The *video adapter* is a circuit card inside the computer that controls the monitor. Its purpose is to generate and maintain the text and graphics that you see on the screen. There are two basic types of video adapters: the monochrome adapter, which can only display text characters in black and white, and the color/graphics adapter, which can display text and graphics in color. Though uncommon, it is possible for both of these adapters to be in your computer. You can use MODE to select a video adapter or set the way that it displays information. The general form of MODE to do this is

MODE *video-mode*

where *video mode* is one of the adapter codes shown in Table 11-2.

If you have a color/graphics adapter, you can set it to either 40- or 80-column mode and to display in either color or black and white. For example, if you have a color/graphics adapter, enter

```
MODE CO40
```

The screen will clear, and you will see the DOS prompt displayed at twice its usual size. In 40-column mode the letters are twice as big, so only 40

Code	Effect
40	Sets a color/graphics adapter display width to 40 columns
80	Sets a color/graphics adapter display width to 80 columns
BW40	Activates the color/graphics adapter and sets the width to 40 columns and the display mode to black and white
BW80	Activates the color/graphics adapter and sets the width to 80 columns and the display mode to black and white
CO40	Activates the color/graphics adapter and sets the width to 40 columns and the display mode to color
CO80	Activates the color/graphics adapter and sets the width to 80 columns and the display mode to color
MONO	Activates the monochrome adapter—the display width is always 80 columns

TABLE 11-2   The MODE Video Codes

can fit from side to side. For this reason, 40-column mode is almost never used. To reset the display to the normal 80-column mode, enter

```
MODE C080
```

If you have a monochrome adapter, you cannot change its mode of operation. However, if you have two adapters in your system, you can enter

```
MODE MONO
```

to switch to the monochrome adapter.

Although fairly rare, there can sometimes be a mismatch between the color/graphics video adapter and the monitor, which causes the image not to be centered (left and right) on the screen. You can shift the display left or right by using the following form of MODE:

MODE *video-adapter, R/L,* T

Use "R" to shift the display to the right or "L" to shift it to the left. The display is shifted two spaces in 80-column mode and one space in 40-column mode. The "T" is optional; when present, it causes a test pattern to be displayed and asks you whether the screen is correct. For example, the following command

```
MODE C080, L, T
```

produces this display:

```
0123456789012334567890 1/.../5678901234567890 1234567890
Do you see the rightmost 9? (Y/N)
```

If you press N, the display is shifted again and you are reprompted.

Setting the Printer

You can set the maximum number of characters per line and the number of lines per vertical inch that the printer will display using the following form of MODE:

MODE LPT#:*length, lines-per-inch*

where the # must be printer number 1, 2, or 3 (there can be up to three printers on the system). The *length* must be either 80 or 132, and *lines-per-inch* must be either 6 or 8. When DOS begins, the line length is 80 with 6 lines per inch. You should understand that when you select 132, the printer automatically makes each character smaller so that 132 characters can fit on one line. Selecting 8 lines per vertical inch simply puts the lines closer together.

Configuring the Serial Port

To transfer data to external devices, a computer can use two types of ports: parallel and serial. The parallel ports are usually used for printers, and the serial ports are used for such things as modems, plotters, and other special devices. However, a printer can be connected to a serial port. The full name for the serial port — and the way it is referred to in the IBM user manuals — is the asynchronous serial communications adapter. But *serial port* is much shorter and is the commonly used term.

The most important difference between the parallel and serial ports is that a parallel port transmits 8 bits of data (1 byte) at a time, while the serial port transmits data 1 bit at a time (hence the name serial). The rate at which the bits are transmitted is measured in *bits per second* and is abbreviated as *baud*. In order for the serial port to communicate with an external device, the baud of the device must match the baud of the serial port. This is usually done for you automatically by the application programs you are using, but you may occasionally be told to manually set the baud. You can do this by using the MODE command with the general form

MODE COM#:*baud*

where # is the adapter number 1 through 4, and *baud* is the baud setting, which must be one of the following numbers: 110, 150, 300, 600, 1200,

2400, 4800, 9600, 19200. The larger the number, the faster the transfer rate. Though only the first two digits are actually necessary, you can use the whole number if you like. For example, to set COM1 to 9600 baud, enter

```
MODE COM1:9600
```

The default setting for the serial ports is 1200 baud.

The serial ports have several other attributes that may need to be set to something other than their default values. Occasionally you may have to set these values. Though it is beyond the scope of this book to explain the technical details of these attributes, we will present a brief overview. A serial port uses one of the following: even, odd, or no parity. The *parity* setting determines if and how error checking will be performed. No parity means that no error checking occurs. The parity of the serial port and the external device communicated with must be the same. The default setting is even. The number of *data bits* determines how many bits are used to transfer information. This number can be either 7 or 8, with the default value being 7. The number of *stop bits* determines how many nondata bits occur between the data bits. This can be either 1 or 2; the default is 2 for 110 baud and 1 for the others. The general form of MODE used to set all the information for the port is

MODE COM#:*baud, parity, data-bits, stop-bits*

where *parity* is "E" for even, "O" for odd, or "N" for none. The *data-bits* and *stop-bits* are numbers. For example, to set the COM1 to 300 baud, even parity, 8 data bits, and 2 stop bits, enter

```
MODE COM1:300, E, 8, 2
```

Finally, if the serial port is to be used with a printer, you should specify the P option. For example, if you have a printer that runs at 9600 baud and uses even parity, 7 data bits, and 1 stop bit, enter

```
MODE COM1:9600, E, 7, 1, P
```

Redirecting Printer Output

If you have a serial printer, you can redirect all printer output to it by using this form of MODE:

MODE LPT#=COM#

where # is the number 1 through 3 for LPT or 1 through 4 for COM. For example, the following command switches the default printer to COM1:

```
MODE LPT1=COM1
```

Now all printer output, including that produced by the PRINT command and the PRINT SCREEN command, will be directed to COM1.

USING THE CONFIG.SYS FILE

DOS has a number of features that can only be set when it begins execution. That is, some aspects of DOS may not be changed once the DOS prompt is displayed because they affect the fundamental operation of the system. To alter these types of attributes, you must use a special configuration file called CONFIG.SYS and some special DOS configuration commands. When DOS begins execution, it looks in the root directory of the disk it loaded from for the file CONFIG.SYS. If it is present, DOS reads the given configuration commands and sets the specified parameters accordingly. If CONFIG.SYS is not found, DOS uses its default settings. When you create or alter the CONFIG.SYS file, none of the changes will take effect until you restart DOS. Some of the commands are intended only for programmers or people specifically in charge of configuring a system and will not be examined. However, we will look at the configuration commands that you may want or need to use.

BREAK

As you know, the CTRL-BREAK key combination is used to cancel a command or application program and return to DOS. However, DOS's default method of operation only checks for a CTRL-BREAK when I/O operations take place to the standard input, output, printer, or serial port. Some programs may not perform any of these operations for quite some time and therefore may not respond quickly to a CTRL-BREAK command. For example, a database program that is doing a sort operation on a very large file may not perform any I/O operations for several minutes. You can instruct DOS to check for a CTRL-BREAK more frequently by placing the following command in the CONFIG.SYS file:

```
BREAK = ON
```

Keep in mind, however, that this will cause all commands and programs to run slower because DOS is spending more time checking to see if you have pressed CTRL-BREAK.

COUNTRY

As you may know, different countries and different languages may vary in how they display and define the time, date, and currency symbols. Also, collating sequence and certain capitalization conventions may differ. For example, in Europe the comma is used as a decimal separator instead of the period. Generally, if you live in a country other than the United States, your computer will, by default, be configured to that country's standards. However, should you need to change DOS to conform to the conventions of a different country, you can use the COUNTRY command to accomplish this. The COUNTRY command takes the general form

COUNTRY = *code*

where code must be one of the codes listed in Table 11-3.

For example, the following command configures DOS for Spain:

```
COUNTRY = 034
```

If the country you want is not listed, you must choose the one whose conventions are the closest to what you need.

Beginning with DOS version 3.30, extended support has been given to countries with special character requirements, and you can specify a character set definition with the COUNTRY command. This issue is covered at the end of this chapter when we discuss foreign language versions of DOS.

DEVICE

The parts of DOS that control the various devices of the computer are called *device drivers*. All the drivers necessary for the operation of a standard configuration of the computer are included in DOS when it begins execution. However, some special device drivers are optional, and you must tell DOS to load them if you want to use them. DOS version 3.30 supplies five additional device drivers:

- ANSI.SYS
- DRIVER.SYS
- PRINTER.SYS
- DISPLAY.SYS
- VDISK.SYS

Also, you may have special hardware requiring special device drivers that are supplied with the equipment. For example, a mouse typically requires a special device driver, usually called MOUSE.SYS.

To tell DOS to load a device driver, use the DEVICE command, which takes the general form

DEVICE = *device-driver*

We will examine the function and use of the DOS device drivers in turn.

ANSI.SYS

Occasionally, an application program will instruct you to load the ANSI.SYS device driver, which enables DOS to understand an additional method of controlling the cursor's position on the screen. It does not give you any more control or command over the screen, but it does make it easier for some types of application programs to use the screen. If you need to load this driver, use the following command in the CONFIG.SYS file:

```
DEVICE = ANSI.SYS
```

Country	Code
Arabic-speaking	785
Australia	061
Belgium	032
Canada — English	001
Canada — French	002
Denmark	045
Finland	358
France	033
Germany	049
Israel — Hebrew	972
Italy	039
Netherlands	031
Norway	047
Portugal	351
South America	003
Spain	034
Sweden	046
Switzerland	041
United Kingdom	044
United States	001

TABLE 11-3   The DOS Country Codes

DRIVER.SYS

DRIVER.SYS is a complicated device driver that alters the way DOS accesses the disk drives of your system. Though most of what the command can do is of interest only to programmers, it has one use that can solve a very perplexing problem. We will examine this form now.

If you have an AT-type computer, the first floppy will probably be a 1.2MB drive. The second floppy, if it exists, can be either a 1.2MB or a 360KB drive. If you have a 360KB as your second drive, how can you copy a 1.2MB diskette? The answer is to tell DOS to assign the A drive a second drive designation, such as D, and then use a command like the following:

```
COPY A:*.* D:
```

Each time the name of the drive is changed, DOS prompts you to strike a key. For example, before switching to D, you will see the following:

```
Insert Diskette for drive D: and strike
any key when ready
```

This allows you to switch diskettes and thus copy a diskette using only one drive. If you have only one floppy, DOS automatically assigns the drive the two names A and B; however, when the second drive exists, DOS does not do this.

To allow drive A to be called by another name, place the following command in your CONFIG.SYS file:

```
DEVICE = DRIVER.SYS /D:C /F:1
```

Depending upon how your system is set up, the second drive name will be the next letter in the alphabet that is not currently assigned. The number after the /F is determined by the following table:

Value	Floppy Drive Type
0	160/180KB
0	320/360KB
1	1.2MB
2	720KB
7	1.44MB

Select the value that suits your needs.

PRINTER.SYS and DISPLAY.SYS

Version 3.30 of DOS added these two device drivers as part of DOS's increased support of non-English-language environments. If you speak English, you will not need to use these drivers. Also, if you live in a non-English-speaking country, your computer is probably already configured for you. Generally, then, you won't have to worry about these device drivers.

VDISK.SYS

The one device driver that you will really want to use is VDISK.SYS, which is used to create a virtual disk drive in RAM (sometimes referred to as a *RAM-disk*). A virtual disk simulates the operation of a disk drive using RAM rather than the magnetic surface of the disk to hold the files. As far as your programs are concerned, a virtual disk looks and acts just like a regular disk drive. However, there is one big difference that you will see and appreciate: virtual disks are much faster than standard disk drives because they run at the speed of the computer's memory, which is always faster than the transfer rate of a disk drive. However, this speed has its price. The virtual disk effectively reduces the amount of available memory of the system. While this is often not a problem, some application programs may require so much memory that a virtual disk cannot be used. You should also be aware that when the power is turned off, or if the computer is restarted, the contents of what is stored in the virtual disk are lost. So be sure to copy files that you wish to save to an actual disk before concluding a session at the computer.

The basic form of the VDISK.SYS command is

DEVICE = VDISK.SYS *total-size sector-size entries*

where *total-size* is the size of the virtual disk in kilobytes. The default value is 64K, but this is usually too small to be of any value. If you specify a value larger than can be allocated, VDISK adjusts it to the largest amount that will fit in memory. The *sector-size* specifies how large to make the sector size and must be 128, 256, or 512 bytes. Real disks use large sector sizes to achieve faster performance, but there is little or no advantage to this on a virtual disk. Therefore, it is best to use the default value of 128 because it makes the most efficient use of memory. The *entries* argument specifies the number of directory entries to be allowed by the virtual disk. This value is 64 by default and is usually a good choice, though you can specify any number between 2 and 512.

For example, the following command in CONFIG.SYS creates a virtual disk 384K bytes in size, uses 128-byte sectors, and has 64 directory entries.

```
DEVICE = VDISK.SYS 384 128 64
```

Several computers have what is called *extended memory,* which is memory that is not directly usable by DOS but may be used by programs running under DOS. If you have extended memory, you can use it for the virtual disk by placing the / E option at the end of the VDISK command. For example, the following command tells VDISK to use the extended memory of the computer.

```
DEVICE - VDISK.SYS 512 128 64 /E
```

When VDISK.SYS is installed during startup, you will see

```
VDISK Version 3.3 virtual disk X
```

where "X" will be the letter of the virtual disk.

Use of a virtual disk is highly recommended because of the dramatic increase in speed.

FILES and FCBS

You can specify the number of files that may concurrently be open and the number of file control blocks (FCBS) that may concurrently be in use. (A *file control block* is a region of memory used by DOS to store information about an open file.) The default values given to these items are acceptable in most cases, but some application programs may require you to change them in order to run correctly.

The number of concurrently open files is 8 by default. If you need to change this, use the FILES command, which has the general form

FILES = *number*

where *number* is a number between 8 and 255. For example, the following command sets the number of files to 10.

```
FILES = 10
```

To change the number of file control blocks, use the FCBS = command, which has the general form

FCBS *total, permanent*

where *total* is the total number of file control blocks. It must be between 1 and 255; the default is 4. The number of file control blocks that DOS may not automatically close is determined by *permanent*. The default value is 0, but it may be between 0 and 255. For example, the following command tells DOS to allow 12 file control blocks and to not automatically close any of them.

```
FCBS=12, 12
```

LASTDRIVE

By default, DOS assumes that the last drive in the system will be E. However, because it is possible to have more drives — especially using virtual disks — you can use the LASTDRIVE command to increase the number of drives allowed. The general form of LASTDRIVE is

LASTDRIVE = *letter*

where *letter* is the drive letter and must be between "A" and "Z."

PATH

Until now, whenever you needed to execute a command or program, the file had to be in the current working directory. However, you can tell DOS to look in other directories for external commands, programs, and batch files by using the PATH command. The general form of PATH is

PATH *path-list*

where *path-list* is a list of paths, separated by a semicolon, that will be searched. You cannot use spaces in the path list.

To understand how PATH works, assume that a disk has the directory structure shown here.

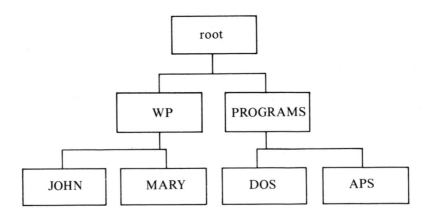

Further assume that all DOS external commands are in the DOS directory and all application programs are in the APS directory. To allow the access of any DOS external command or application program from any directory, enter

```
PATH \PROGRAMS\DOS;\PROGRAMS\APS
```

Now, whenever a command is given to DOS that is not internal, DOS will first check the current directory. If it is not found, DOS then begins checking, in order, those directories specified by the PATH command, beginning with the \PROGRAMS \DOS directory. If the command is not found there, DOS then searches the \PROGRAMS \APS directory.

To see what the current path is, simply enter PATH with no arguments. To reset the path to its default, enter

```
PATH ;
```

Remember, setting a search path with PATH causes DOS to search the specified directories only for .EXE, .COM, and .BAT files. You cannot access data files with the PATH command.

APPEND

Beginning with version 3.20, DOS now includes the APPEND command, which gives you access to files in other directories and operates much like PATH except that it works with any type of file. The general form of APPEND is

APPEND *path-list*

where *path-list* is a semicolon-separated list of paths. APPEND is both an internal and external command. The first time that APPEND is executed, it is loaded from disk. Afterward, however, it becomes part of DOS's internal commands. As with PATH, there can be no spaces in the path list.

Assume the same directory structure that we used with the PATH command. APPEND allows you to access data files in the JOHN and MARY directories:

```
APPEND \WP\JOHN;\WP\MARY
```

Now the data files in these directories can be accessed from any other directory. However, they will not show up in a directory listing of any other directory. Nor can you execute commands or programs in the appended directory.

To see which directories are currently appended to the current one, enter APPEND with no arguments. To cancel an APPEND, enter

```
APPEND ;
```

You can give APPEND the ability to show files in the appended directory when the current directory is listed, and to execute external commands and programs, by specifying the /X option *the first time* that APPEND is executed. That is, the first time that you execute APPEND, enter

```
APPEND /X
```

and then enter the APPEND command you want. Now the files in the appended directories will show when the current directory is listed, and you may execute commands and programs found in the appended directories.

At this point you might be tempted to simply APPEND all directories together so that you can reach any file in any directory at any time. But this is a bad idea for two reasons. First, it negates the basic philosphy of tree-structured directories and can easily make it impossible for you to correctly manage your files. Second, although you can read a file from any directory, if an application program writes a file, it will be written in the current directory. This means that if you edit a file in the JOHN directory while the current directory is MARY, then saving that file writes it to MARY, leaving the original version in JOHN unchanged.

ASSIGN

You can cause DOS to reroute an I/O request for one drive to another by using the ASSIGN command. For example, you can make all disk I/O options that specify drive A actually go to drive B. The general form of ASSIGN is

ASSIGN *old-drive* = *new-drive*

ASSIGN is an external command.

If you have two floppy drives, try the following command:

```
ASSIGN A = B
```

Now put your DOS work disk in B and enter

```
DIR A:
```

As you can see, the B drive is activated.

If you have a fixed disk, put a DOS diskette in A and try this sequence of commands:

```
ASSSIGN C = A
DIR C:
```

This activates the A drive.

You can specify more than one drive reassignment at a time. For example, the following command switches drives A and B:

```
ASSIGN A = B   B = A
```

To reset the drive assignments to their original values, enter ASSIGN with no arguments.

The ASSIGN command's principal use is to allow application programs originally written under the assumption that the computer would have two floppy drives called A and B to take advantage of a fixed disk.

SUBST

The external command SUBST lets you specify a drive specifier that may refer to either another drive or a directory. This drive specifier is conceptually similar to a nickname. SUBST has the general form

SUBST *nickname: drive-name:* \path

where *nickname* is the new drive letter that can be used to refer to *drive-name* \path. For example, the following command allows you to refer to the A drive as E (as well as A).

```
SUBST E: A:\
```

You can also substitute a drive specifier for a subdirectory that is on the same disk. For example, assume the directory structure below on drive C:

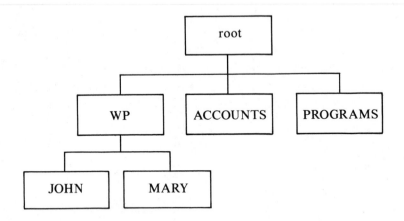

After executing the following command,

```
SUBST E: E:\WP\MARY
```

you may now refer to the \WP \MARY directory as if it were drive E.

The drive letter that you select as a nickname must be less than or equal to E unless you have used a LASTDRIVE command to the contrary in your CONFIG.SYS file.

You can display the current substitutions by entering SUBST with no arguments. If substitution of E for \WP \MARY has been made, for example, SUBST will display the following:

```
E: => C:\WP\MARY
```

To remove a substitution, use the general form

SUBST *nickname* /D

The SUBST command exists to allow application programs to be used that do not recognize path names. Although most programs available today recognize the full DOS path name, very early programs did not. But these early programs do recognize drive specifiers, so you can use SUBST as a way of making a program work correctly with directories.

However, the likelihood of your coming across a program that does not recognize path names is becoming increasingly low.

JOIN

The JOIN command allows the directory of one disk to be connected to a directory on a different disk so that the second directory can access the first disk's files. JOIN is an external command with the general form

JOIN *first-drive joined-drive \directory*

where *first-drive* is the drive specifier of the drive that will be joined to *joined-drive* as directory *directory*.

For example, the following command joins the A drive to the B drive in the directory B: \ADRIVE.

```
JOIN A: B:\ADRIVE
```

If drive B is made current, a directory listing will show the directory ADRIVE. You can switch to this directory the way you switch to other directories by using the CD command. To put it differently, after the preceding JOIN command, all references to files on A will be made as if they are in the ADRIVE directory of B.

You can see what is joined to what by entering JOIN with no arguments. To cancel a joining, use the general form

JOIN *first-drive* / D

JOIN has a number of restrictions to its use. The directory name that you specify for access to the joined drive must be empty or nonexistent. You cannot join the currently selected drive because the drive name for the joining drive becomes invalid immediately following the JOIN command. Further, do not use JOIN if SUBST or ASSIGN has been used on either of the drives participating in the command. Finally, do not use the BACKUP, DISKCOPY, FORMAT, RESTORE, or DISKCOMP command when one drive has been joined to another.

INTERNATIONAL CONFIGURATIONS

As you learned when reading about the CONFIG.SYS file, several conventions differ among countries, such as how the time, date, and currency symbols are defined. However, beyond that, several non-English languages require some additional characters, some accented characters, or both. Also, the exact layout of the keyboard will differ because of the inclusion of these different characters. (For the keyboard layouts for other countries and languages, refer to your DOS manual.) DOS allows you to change the configuration of the keyboard and which characters are actually displayed through the use of the KEYB command. However, its operation differs substantially between DOS versions prior to 3.30 and DOS version 3.30 or greater. Both will be considered here.

Keep in mind that configuring DOS for a language other than English *does not* cause DOS to translate any messages—all DOS prompts remain in English.

KEYB Prior to Version 3.30

For versions of DOS prior to 3.30, five external commands called KEYBFR, KEYBGR, KEYBIT, KEYBSP, and KEYBUK correspond to France, Germany, Italy, Spain, and the United Kingdom. To select the keyboard layout and character set for one of those countries, simply enter the proper command. You might want to try executing KEYBFR at this time. When you press the A key, you will see a "Q" printed! On the French keyboard layout, the positions of the "A" and "Q" are reversed.

You can switch back to the U.S.-style keyboard at any time by pressing CTRL, ALT, F1. To go back to the other language, press CTRL, ALT, F2.

The KEYB Command in DOS Version 3.30 and Greater

DOS version 3.30 has expanded (and greatly complicated) multinational support capabilities. Essentially, a completely new approach has been established that lets more countries use the default settings. Fortunately, if you live in one of these countries, switching the keyboard and character layout is just as simple as it was under earlier versions of DOS. However, if you live in an area not supported by the default settings, a rather lengthy and complex set of command sequences is necessary to establish the proper keyboard and character set.

DOS version 3.30 has added several files with the extension .CPI. These are *code page information* files, which hold the codes for the various keyboard and printer character sets. Table 11-4 shows the countries supported along with their keyboard and code page codes.

If you live in a country that uses code page 437, you needn't worry about code page switching. If you do not, refer to your DOS user manual for explicit instructions on how to switch to the proper code page. (Generally, if you live in one of these countries, your computer will be

Country	Keyboard Code	Code Page Code
Australia	US	437
Belgium	BE	437
Canada — English	US	437
Canada — French	CF	863
Denmark	DK	865
Finland	SU	437
France	FR	437
Germany	GR	437
Italy	IT	437
Latin America	LA	437
Netherlands	NL	437
Norway	NO	865
Portugal	PO	860
Spain	SP	437
Sweden	SV	437
Switzerland — French	SF	437
Switzerland — German	SG	437
United Kingdom	UK	437
United States	US	437

From *Disk Operating System 3.30 Reference*, page 9-7. Courtesy of International Business Machines Corporation.

TABLE 11-4   Countries Supported with Keyboard and Code Page Codes

preconfigured for you, and you won't need to worry about it.)

Although you probably don't have to use code page switching, you will still need to use a slightly different form of the KEYB command than the one described for versions of DOS prior to 3.30. The general form of the KEYB command is

KEYB *keyboard code-page path*

where *keyboard* is a keyboard code for the country desired, *code-page* is the proper code page, and *path* is the path to the KEYBOARD.SYS file. You don't usually specify the last two arguments, allowing them to default to the current code page and the root directory. For example, to switch to a French-style keyboard, enter the following command:

```
KEBY FR
```

You should try this now. Notice that the positions of the "A" and the "Q" are reversed on the French keyboard. You can switch back to the U.S.-style keyboard at any time by pressing CTRL, ALT, F1. To return to the other language, press CTRL, ALT, F2.

Using SELECT to Prepare Foreign Versions of DOS

You can use the SELECT command to prepare a DOS diskette that is automatically configured for a foreign country. The most common form of SELECT is

SELECT A: B: *country keyboard*

where *country* is one of the country codes defined in Table 11-3 and *keyboard* is one of the keyboard codes shown in Table 11-4. This command will format the disk in B, copy DOS to that disk, and then prepare the necessary CONFIG.SYS and AUTOEXEC.BAT files for the specified country and keyboard. It requires that a DOS disk be in A. If you have only one drive, you will have to swap diskettes as prompted by DOS. For example, the following command creates a DOS diskette for Germany:

```
SELECT A: B: 049 GR
```

When SELECT begins, it displays the following warning and prompt:

```
SELECT is used to install DOS the first
time.  SELECT erases everything on the
specified target and then installs DOS.
Do you want to continue (Y/N)?
```

Upon completion, the destination diskette will contain a CONFIG.SYS file containing

```
COUNTRY=049,437
```

and an AUTOEXEC.BAT file containing

```
PATH \;
KEYB GR 049
ECHO OFF
DATE
TIME
VER
```

Now, whenever you want to use DOS in its German version, simply start the system with the German diskette. To go back to English, use the standard DOS diskette to restart the computer.

SUMMARY

In this chapter you learned a number of ways to configure your system, including

- The DOS prompt
- Using the MODE command
- Creating a CONFIG.SYS file
- Setting up a virtual disk
- Using PATH and APPEND
- Changing the way that DOS accesses the disk drives
- Creating international diskettes

In the next chapter you will learn about managing your disks.

12

FLOPPY-DISK MANAGEMENT

Aside from the invention of the microprocessor that makes personal computers possible, no device has contributed as much to the development and success of the microcomputer as the floppy disk drive. The reasons for this are threefold. First, floppy disk drives are inexpensive compared to fixed disks (though fixed disks are cheaper in terms of bytes of storage per dollar). In the early days of microcomputers, a fixed disk could easily cost several thousand dollars, while a floppy drive might sell for just a few hundred. Second, compared to the only other cheap method of data storage — cassette tape — floppy disks are fast. Finally, the floppy disk gives users an easy and inexpensive way to share programs and transfer files. (Also, software developers found floppy diskettes the perfect medium on which to sell their programs.) For these reasons, the floppy disk has earned a lasting place in the world of computing.

How the floppy disk is used depends upon whether it is the main disk of the system or only a companion to a fixed disk. In a great many fixed-disk systems the floppy disk is no longer the main disk drive. In fact, in most such systems, the floppy is used for only two purposes: (1) to back up information on the fixed disk for offsite storage, and (2) to put programs or files onto the fixed disk. However, in non-fixed-disk systems the floppy drive is used as the main storage device. In this chapter we will concentrate primarily on the floppy disk as it is used in non-fixed-disk systems. Its use as a backup for the fixed disk is covered in Chapter 13.

One last point: in floppy-only systems one drive is seldom practical; at least two are required. Much of the material in this chapter assumes that at least two floppy drives are present.

BALANCING DOS AND APPLICATIONS ON YOUR WORK DISK

As you probably know, a diskette containing DOS and all its external commands can leave very little extra room for your files. However, you usually do not need most of the external commands and miscellaneous files when you are using your application programs. Therefore you can free a lot of room on your DOS/application work disk by erasing the commands and files that you don't use frequently. (Remember, don't delete files on your master DOS diskette.) Figure 12-1 shows a list of all the files supplied with version 3.30 of DOS.

Let's look at which files it makes sense to eliminate and in which situations they can be eliminated.

4201	CPI
5202	CPI
ANSI	SYS
APPEND	EXE
ASSIGN	COM
ATTRIB	EXE
BACKUP	COM
BASIC	COM
BASIC	PIF
BASICA	COM
BASICA	PIF
CHKDSK	COM
COMMAND	COM

FIGURE 12-1 Commands and files supplied in DOS version 3.30

COMP	COM
COUNTRY	SYS
DEBUG	COM
DISKCOMP	COM
DISKCOPY	COM
DISPLAY	SYS
DRIVER	SYS
EDLIN	COM
EGA	CPI
FASTOPEN	EXE
FDISK	COM
FIND	EXE
FORMAT	COM
GRAFTABL	COM
GRAPHICS	COM
JOIN	EXE
KEYB	COM
KEYBOARD	SYS
LABEL	COM
LCD	CPI
MODE	COM
MORE	COM
MORTGAGE	BAS
NLSFUNC	EXE
PRINT	COM
PRINTER	SYS
RECOVER	COM
REPLACE	EXE
RESTORE	COM
SELECT	COM
SHARE	EXE
SORT	EXE
SUBST	EXE
SYS	COM
TREE	COM
VDISK	SYS
XCOPY	EXE

FIGURE 12-1   Commands and files supplied in DOS version 3.30 (*continued*)

U.S. English-Language Usage

If you speak English and use your computer in the United States, you can eliminate the following files, which are used to support foreign languages and countries:

4201.CPI
5201.CPI
COUNTRY.SYS
DISPLAY.SYS
EGA.CPI
KEYB.SYS
KEYBOARD.SYS
LCD.CPI
NLSFUNC.EXE
PRINTER.SYS

If you live in a country other than the United States, you can still probably eliminate all but COUNTRY.SYS. (See the section in Chapter 11 on multinational versions of DOS.)

Removing Device Drivers

If you don't need them, you can remove the following device drivers:

ANSI.SYS
DRIVER.SYS
VDISK.SYS

REMOVING FORMATTING AND DOS TRANSFER COMMANDS

On a work disk, you will probably not need any of the commands that are used to create new disks or install DOS. You will usually perform such tasks with your DOS disk rather than an application work disk. If this is the case, you can erase the following files:

FDISK.COM
FORMAT.COM
SELECT.COM
SYS.COM

Programmer-Related Commands

Unless you are a programmer, you can remove the following files:

BASIC.COM
BASIC.PIF
BASICA.COM
BASICA.PIF
DEBUG.COM
MORTGAGE.BAS

Fixed-Disk Commands

If you don't have a fixed disk, you can erase the following commands:

BACKUP.COM
FASTOPEN.EXE
RESTORE.COM

Seldom-Used Commands

You will probably never use the following commands:

APPEND.EXE
ASSIGN.COM
ATTRIB.EXE
GRAFTABL.COM
JOIN.EXE
SUBST.EXE

If this is the case, remove them from your application work disk. In general, you can remove any command that you do not use.

The best way to balance the needs of DOS and those of your application essentially is to let the diskette in drive A hold DOS while you use the one in B to hold your application programs and files.

FLOPPY DISKS AND SUBDIRECTORIES

Because of the limited storage on a floppy diskette, subdirectories are seldom used because it is easier (or necessary) to simply keep logically separate applications on separate diskettes. However, we don't mean to discourage you from creating and using subdirectories with your floppies. If you do use subdirectories on floppies, you should be aware of two performance issues.

First, each additional level of subdirectories increases the access time to the files in those subdirectories. On fixed disks this extra time is not much of an issue because they are so much faster than floppy drives.

However, on floppies this additional access time can become annoying. So use heavily nested subdirectories only when you can justify them.

Second, each subdirectory uses disk space to hold its directory entries. Because space on a floppy is already limited, an unwarranted number of subdirectories could seriously decrease the amount of information that you could store on the disk.

BACKING UP FLOPPY DISKS

If you do not have a fixed disk, you must back up the floppy disks that contain your application programs and data on a regular basis. To put it bluntly, not making copies of important data is negligence of the highest order.

Sources of Data Loss

Before discussing the backup routine, let's look at the four ways that valuable data can be destroyed.

Computer Failure   The least common way that important information can be destroyed on a diskette is through computer failure. Few machine errors will destroy a file. But if the software that accesses the information is writing to the disk when a hardware failure occurs, data could be destroyed. The most common causes of hardware failures are static electricity, overheating, line current transients, and physical abuse. Age is not as significant a factor in hardware failures as it once was because the integrated circuits now used to construct the computer have a very long mean time to failure.

It is very difficult to guard against machine errors except by trying to maintain a clean environment and a steady source of power. If power transients are a problem in your area, you might want to invest in a surge protector.

Medium Failures   The next least frequent source of data loss is physical destruction of the magnetic medium of the floppy disk. This can result from negligence on the part of the user or from a poorly manufactured diskette that simply disintegrates. Fortunately, with care, floppy diskettes tend to last a long time. However, any diskette that has been in heavy daily service for more than a year is a good candidate for replacement.

Software Errors   Programmers are not perfect. Hence your application programs could contain one or more errors capable of destroying information. For the user who is not computer knowledgeable, it is sometimes difficult to distinguish between software and hardware errors. However, if data is consistently lost when you perform the same sequence of actions, software is likely the culprit.

Often you can work with the developers of your application software to get these errors fixed. If not, you must find different, more reliable, programs to use.

Human Error   Computers are one of the most reliable devices in use. People are not! The accidental erasing of important data is epidemic. Frankly, there is no way to guard against it —it is simply too easy to erase a file.

The Backup Routine

Your only protection against having the data on a diskette destroyed is the *backup routine*. As you will come to understand, it is not enough just to make copies of important diskettes. *When* to make them, *how many* to maintain, and how to *recover* from a loss are also crucial.

Many data processing managers recommend the *rotating triad* method of backup. With this method, you have three backup diskettes for every work disk. The first, called the *daily backup,* is used to back up the work disk on a daily basis. Actually, you may find that it is better to back up after a shorter period, such as every two hours, if your data is volatile. The daily disk substitutes for the work disk should failure occur. (Actually, a copy of it should be used, but we will discuss recover shortly.)

The next disk in the triad is the *weekly backup*. Every Friday at 5 P.M., the contents of the daily disk are copied to the weekly disk. Thus, if both the master work disk and the daily disk are destroyed, the weekly disk can be used as a fairly close starting point.

At the end of each month, the weekly backup is *retired* and put in a safe place. A new copy of the daily disk is made and becomes the next month's weekly backup. The retired monthly backup completes the triad. In this way, if an error is not discovered for some time and has already corrupted the daily and weekly disks, the monthly backup can be used.

Because the nearest backup is potentially one month out of date, some managers employ the *snapshot* method in addition to the rotating triad. With this method, four diskettes are created for each work disk and are labeled One through Four. Every Wednesday, a copy of the daily disk is placed on one of the snapshot diskettes, beginning with One the first week, Two the second week, and so on. After Four has been used, the process cycles back to One. In this way an error will not perpetuate itself through all the diskettes.

Backing Up a Disk

The best way to back up a diskette is by using DISKCOPY. Using COPY or even XCOPY is not as good because it permits human error —you could forget to copy a file or two.

Recovering Data

If you have to go to a backup diskette, use it only to make a copy; then use the copy. If a hardware or software problem has caused the loss of a file, it could happen again. You can never risk the destruction of a backup diskette. Be sure to write-protect the disk before putting it in the computer.

Remember also to restore all files even if only one is lost because many application programs use two or more files that work together. If these files are out of synchronization, you could be heading for even more trouble.

MAILING DISKETTES

To close this chapter, a few words about how to mail or ship floppy disks are in order. The best way to mail a diskette is in a diskette mailer. If none is available, however, place the diskette between two strong pieces of cardboard and put it in a large envelope. Be sure to write on the package, in large letters, that a floppy diskette is enclosed and should not be bent.

SUMMARY

In this chapter you learned

- How to free space on your DOS work diskette
- The effects of subdirectories on floppy disks
- How to maintain a backup routine
- How to mail a diskette

In the next chapter you will learn to manage and back up your fixed disk.

13

FIXED-DISK
MANAGEMENT

With storage capabilities in excess of 70 megabytes, the fixed disk is a system resource that demands attention. Actually, most business users will not consider buying a computer without a fixed disk, and many home users find that compared to floppies, the extra storage and speed of the fixed disk are worth the extra expense. In this chapter you will learn some valuable techniques to help you manage this important device.

HOW FIXED AND FLOPPY DISKS DIFFER

The most fundamental difference between fixed and floppy disks is that the fixed disk, unlike the floppy, is not removable from the drive. It is not removable for two main reasons. First, the read/write head is mounted very close to the surface of the disk and is fairly delicate. Second, even if the drive head were retracted to a safe position, the fixed disk is very easily harmed by dust, so just opening its case is a bad idea.

From the aspect of performance, the fixed disk typically runs 10 times faster than a floppy and stores from 10 to 200 times as much information. It is the increased storage, however, that really distinguishes how fixed disks tend to be used. Unlike floppies, a fixed disk tends to have a complex directory structure that holds a wide range of information and application programs. In a way, a floppy disk is like a single-family dwelling, while a fixed disk is like a high-rise condominium.

BACKING UP YOUR FIXED DISK

Making and maintaining copies of the information on your fixed disk is seldom as easy as it is with floppy disks because of the amount of information usually found on the fixed disk. Unless you have some sort of tape backup system attached to your computer, you cannot copy an entire fixed disk the way you can copy an entire floppy. Instead, you will need to copy the information on the fixed disk to several floppy diskettes. The trouble is that often even one directory on a fixed disk will contain more information than will fit on a single floppy. With only the copying commands you have learned so far, there is no easy and trouble-free way to back up a hard disk. Instead, you must use DOS's external BACKUP command.

The BACKUP command has several forms and numerous options. In this book we will examine the most common forms. All the examples use drive A as the floppy drive receiving the information, though you may substitute drive B if you wish. Drive C is assumed to be the fixed disk. You should substitute the correct drive letter if necessary. BACKUP has the general form

BACKUP *source target options*

where *source* specifies the drive, path, and file names to be copied to *target*.

The number of diskettes that you will need is directly related to the amount of information on your fixed disk. Sometimes this number can be quite large. For example, a full 10-megabyte fixed disk in an IBM XT will require 25 diskettes. However, a full 20-megabyte diskette in an AT using 1.2-megabyte floppies will require only about 20 diskettes. To compute the number of diskettes that you will need, run CHKDSK to find the total storage size, in bytes, of the fixed disk and the amount of free storage. Subtract the amount of free storage from the total storage and then divide this number by the storage size of the floppy drive that you will be using for backups. Rounding this number upward tells you the number of diskettes required. This formula in mathematical notation is

num-diskettes = (total-free)/size of floppy

You must number your backup diskettes because you will have to insert them in order. The exact order in which the diskettes are written is very important because a large file may be spread across two or more diskettes.

Backing Up the Entire Fixed Disk

The most important and by far most common backup scenario is backing up the entire contents of the fixed disk. This is the safest way to ensure that all the data on the disk is copied. To back up the contents of the fixed disk, use the following form of BACKUP, being sure to use only formatted diskettes.

```
BACKUP C:\*.* A: /S
```

The path \ ensures that the backup will begin with the root directory, and the /S option specifies that all subdirectories will be copied. As the backup procedure begins, you will see this message:

```
Insert backup diskette 01 in drive A:

Warning! Files in the target drive
A:\ root directory will be erased
Strike any key when ready

*** Backing up files to drive A: ***
```

As BACKUP continues, you will be prompted to insert additional diskettes until all the information on C has been backed up.

With the form of BACKUP just described, you must use formatted diskettes. However, you can tell BACKUP to format each diskette prior to copying information to it by using the /F option, as shown here.

```
BACKUP C:\*.* A: /S /F
```

This option is available only in versions equal to or greater than 3.30. This approach is generally faster than first formatting several diskettes and then using BACKUP.

Backing Up Portions of the Fixed Disk

In situations where several people use the same computer, it may make more sense for each user to back up his or her own directories rather than the entire disk. For example, assume that the directory structure shown below exists on a fixed disk.

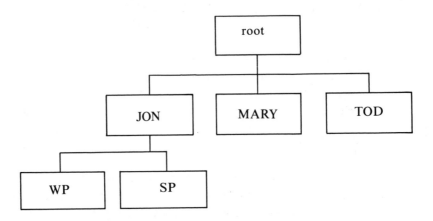

The command that Jon will use to back up his workspace, including the JON directory and its two subdirectories, is

```
BACKUP C:\JON\*.* A: /S
```

In general, you specify a path to the directory where you wish to start the backup.

If you leave off the /S, then only the contents of the directory explicitly specified are copied. For example, the command

```
BACKUP C:\JON\*.* A:
```

copies only the contents of the JON directory and not its subdirectories WP and SP.

Adding Files to Backup Diskettes

The forms of the BACKUP command shown so far erase any previously existing contents of the target diskettes. However, suppose that you perform a complete fixed-disk backup only once a week, and you have simply added three files while leaving the others unchanged. How can you add these files to the backup diskettes without having to recopy the entire fixed disk? The answer is to use BACKUP's /A (add) option. When you specify this option, the target diskettes are not overwritten — rather, the specified files are added to them. For example, to add the file FORMLET.WP to backup diskettes for Jon, enter

```
BACKUP C:\JON\WP\FORMLET.WP A: /A
```

When this command begins execution, you will see the following:

```
Insert last backup diskette in drive A:
Strike any key when ready
```

As is implied by this message, new files are added to the last diskette used by the previous backup.

Backing Up Files Modified on or After a Specified Date

You can back up only those files that have been changed on or after a specified date by using the /D: option. For example, the following command copies those files that have been changed on or after 5-7-87.

```
BACKUP C:\*.* A: /D:5-7-87
```

The format of the date is determined by the country specified with the COUNTRY command in the CONFIG.SYS file, or as mm-dd-yy (standard U.S. format) if no other country is specified.

Keep in mind that use of the /D: option does not prevent the target diskette(s) from being overwritten. To add new files with dates after a certain date, also add the /A option to the command line. For example, the following command will add any new files modified after 5-7-87 to the target diskette(s).

```
BACKUP C:\*.* A: /D:5-7-87 /A
```

Backing Up Files Modified on or After a Specified Time

You can tell BACKUP to copy only those files with times equal to or later than a specified time on a specified date by using the /T: option along with the /D: option. For example, the following command only backs up those files created after 12 noon on 5-7-87.

```
BACKUP C:\*.* A: /D:5-7-87   /T:12:00
```

Again, the format for the date and time will vary in countries other than the United States. Remember, the existing set of backup diskettes will be overwritten.

Backing Up Only Files That Have Changed

By using the /M option, you can tell BACKUP to copy only those files that have changed since the last backup. As you will recall from Chapter 9, all files have an associated archive attribute that can be either on or off. If the archive attribute is on, it indicates that the file has been modified. The BACKUP command automatically turns off the archive attribute. Therefore only files that have been changed will actually be copied. For example, the following command backs up only the modified files of the fixed disk.

```
BACKUP C:\*.* A: /M /S
```

Adding a Log File

With the /L: option, you can have a record of the time and date of the backup, the path and file name of each file backed up, and the number of the diskette that each file is on. You can specify a file name for the log file. If none is specified, BACKUP.LOG is used and is placed in the root directory of both the source and target. If the specified file exists, information is appended to the end. If it does not exist, then the file is created. For example, the following command writes to the file called MYLOG.

```
BACKUP C:\*.* A: /S /L:MYLOG
```

This command uses the default BACKUP.LOG file.

```
BACKUP C:/*.* A: /S /L
```

If DOS is installed in the root directory (as it probably will be) of the fixed disk, then the first line of each entry will contain the date and time of the backup. Each subsequent line lists the disk number and file name.

```
3-22-1987  13:45:51
001 \IBMBIO.COM
001 \IBMDOS.COM
001 \COMMAND.COM
001 \CONFIG.SYS
001 \AUTOEXEC.BAT
```

The log file provides a record of which backup diskette any specific

Option	Meaning
/A	Add files instead of overwriting the backup diskettes
/D	Copy files with dates on or after the specified date
/F	Format each backup diskette before writing to it
/L	Create a log file
/M	Copy only those files that have been created or changed since the last backup
/S	Back up all subdirectories starting with the specified path
/T	Copy files with times equal to or later than the one specified on the given date

TABLE 13-1   The BACKUP Options

file is on. This can speed up the process of restoring a file, as you will shortly see.

Backing Up Floppies with BACKUP

You can use BACKUP to back up the contents of a floppy disk, although this is rarely done because DISKCOPY is clearly superior. However, you can specify any target and any source drive that you desire (except that they cannot be the same drive) as arguments to BACKUP.

Table 13-1 shows a summary of BACKUP's options.

RESTORING FILES

If a file is lost on your fixed disk, you will need to restore it from the backups that you made with BACKUP by using the RESTORE command. Assuming that you are restoring to a fixed disk, the general form of the RESTORE command is

RESTORE *backup fixed options*

where *backup* is one or more of the backup diskettes created using BACKUP and *fixed* denotes the drive, path, and file name specifiers that tell where information will be written to the fixed disk.

During the restoration process, you will be prompted to insert one or more of the backup diskettes beginning with diskette number 1. When you restore the entire fixed disk, all backup diskettes will be read in order. If only certain files are being restored, RESTORE will search through the backup diskettes until it finds them. The RESTORE prompt tells you which diskette to insert next and waits until you press a key. The first prompt will look like this:

```
Insert backup diskette 01 in drive A:
Strike any key when ready
```

Keep in mind that restoring a file means overwriting any existing file with the same name, so use the RESTORE command carefully.

Restoring the Entire Fixed Disk

To restore all the files on the fixed disk, you must have backup diskettes containing all these files. That is, you must have recently used a BACKUP command similar to the following:

```
BACKUP C:\*.* A: /S
```

With the diskettes that hold the backed up information, you should use the following form of the RESTORE command to restore all the files.

```
RESTORE A: C:\*.* /S
```

The /S option tells RESTORE to restore all files and subdirectories. Notice that you specify the path name for where the files will be placed on the fixed disk, not from where they are stored on the backup diskettes.

In general, there are only two occasions when you will completely restore a disk. The first, and most unfortunate, is when a hardware error destroys your fixed disk and a new one is put in the system. In this case you must reload all your files. If you have been following a proper backup procedure (such as the one described later in this chapter), then the disruption should be minimal. However, if the fixed disk crashes and your backups are either out of date or nonexistent, you are probably in for a very painful experience.

The other time that you will want to fully recover a fixed disk is when you are bringing up another system that is intended to have the same function as the first.

Restoring Individual Files

To restore individual files, you must specify the complete path and file names. RESTORE accepts wildcards, so it is possible to restore groups of files.

For example, to restore the files LETTER.ONE, LETTER.TWO, and FORMLET.ONE found in the JON \WP directory, use the following commands.

```
RESTORE A: C:\JON\WP\LETTER.*
RESTORE A: C:\JON\WP\FORMLET.ONE
```

Restoring Files by Date and Time

RESTORE can restore files modified on or *before* a certain date when you add the /B: option. Alternately, the /A: option allows you to restore files that have been modified on or *after* the specified date. For example, the following commands restore all files changed before or on 3-3-89, and after 3-3-88 — a period of one year.

```
RESTORE A: C:*.* /S /B:3-3-89 /A:3-3-88
```

In like fashion you can use /L: to restore those files modified *at or later* than a certain time on a given date, and /E: to restore all files modified *at or prior* to the specified time on a given date. For example, the following commands restore all files modified on 2-28-88 after 12 noon but earlier than 5:01 that afternoon.

```
RESTORE A: C:*.* /S /D:2-28-88 /L:12:00 /E:17:00
```

Restoring Modified Files

The /M option lets you restore only those files that have been modified or deleted from the fixed disk since the last backup was made. For example, the following command restores all files in the WP directory that have been changed.

```
RESTORE A: C:\JON\WP\*.* /M
```

The RESTORE command simply checks the archive attribute of each file and restores those that have it turned on.

Similarly, you can use the /N option to restore only those files that have been deleted from the fixed disk.

Prompted Restoration

If you specify the /P option, RESTORE will prompt you with

```
Warning! File X
was changed after it was backed up
Replace the file (Y/N)?
```

whenever a file on the fixed disk has been changed since the last time it was backed up.

Special Considerations When Using RESTORE

RESTORE does not restore the files BIMBIO.COM, IBMDOS.COM, and COMMAND.COM. You should use the SYS command for the first two and COPY for COMMAND.COM.

You must always start with diskette number 1 to recover a file unless you have created a log file during backup that will tell you the number of the diskette that the file is on.

Files stored on backup diskettes are not the same as standard DOS files. Don't try to use the COPY command to restore files.

The RESTORE options are summarized in Table 13-2.

THE BACKUP ROUTINE FOR FIXED DISKS

The basic philosophy for backing up the fixed disk is the same as for floppy disks. You should still use the rotating triad method of backup; that is, you should maintain daily, weekly, and monthly backup diskettes. (The rotating triad backup method was discussed in Chapter 12.) The only difference is that you will be using many more diskettes for each phase.

Option	Meaning
/A	Restore all files modified on or after the specified date
/B	Restore all files modified on or before the specified date
/E	Restore all files modified at or earlier than the specified time on a given date
/L	Restore all files modified at or later than the specified time on a given date
/M	Restore all files that have been modified or deleted since the last backup
/N	Restore only those files that do not exist on the fixed disk
/P	Prompt before restoring a file
/S	Restore all subdirectories

TABLE 13-2   The RESTORE Options

Because backing up a fixed disk that contains a lot of information is a lengthy process, after an initial backup, you should use the /M option to copy only those files that have changed to the daily backup disks, and then perform a full backup procedure at the end of the week. This will save you time and still ensure the protection of the files.

Because the nearest backup is potentially one month out of date, you should use the snapshot method of backup (described in Chapter 12) in addition to the rotating triad. In this way an error will not perpetuate itself through all the diskettes.

Who Is Responsible?

Someone must be in charge of backing up a fixed disk if the system is used by many people. This may sound simple, but the failure to do this is a major cause of backup diskettes being woefully out of date. When no single person is responsible, everyone assumes that someone else is doing the backups. If you are a manager, make sure that someone's job description includes backing up the fixed disk.

USING FASTOPEN

Starting with DOS version 3.30, the external command FASTOPEN has been included. Its purpose is to allow DOS to quickly access files that are several levels of subdirectories deep. For somewhat technical reasons, it normally takes DOS a lot longer to reach a file with a long path name than to reach one in the root. However, FASTOPEN allows DOS to remember the location of a file and therefore makes accessing that file much faster. The general form of FASTOPEN is

FASTOPEN *drive-specifier=num*

where *drive-specifier* is the name of the drive to which the FASTOPEN command applies. You can use FASTOPEN to provide fast access to the files on only one drive in the system. The optional *num* argument specifies the number of files and directories that FASTOPEN can remember and must be between 10 and 999. If *num* is not present, the default is 34. There can be no spaces between the drive specifier, the equal sign, and the number.

For example, the following command gives fast access to the files on drive C and allows 34 files and/or directories to have fast access.

`FASTOPEN C:`

FASTOPEN will display this message:

`FASTOPEN installed`

The following command allows the last 50 files and/or directories to be remembered.

`FASTOPEN C:=50`

You will usually want to use the default setting for the number of files or directories. For technical reasons, making it too large could actually increase rather than decrease access time. If you make it too small, you will not receive any benefit from it.

FASTOPEN installs itself the first time it is invoked, which means that you can execute it only once. For this reason, you should put it in an AUTOEXEC.BAT file.

LOADING APPLICATIONS TO THE FIXED DISK

No hard and fast rules apply to every situation involving loading applications to the fixed disk. However, some general guidelines will help you make the right decisions. We will examine these here.

Use Subdirectories

The first and most important rule is that each separate application should be loaded into its own directory. Do not put all applications into the root directory. If you do this, not only will the root directory become unmanageable, you will eventually run out of directory entries. It is also not wise to place all applications into one general-purpose applications directory because, again, that directory will become unmanageable.

For example, imagine that you have three applications: a spreadsheet, a word processor, and an inventory package. You should create three subdirectories, with descriptive names such as SPSHT, WP, and INVENT, and place the files associated with each application area into their respective directories.

Sometimes you will add an application that is really a subsystem of an already existing application. For example, if you add a spelling checker to the word processor, it does not make sense to create a new subdirectory off the root for it. Instead, you should simply add it to the WP directory because it is dependent upon the word processor. In certain situations it might be a good idea to place it in a subdirectory of WP. In general, when one application depends on another, put the dependent one in the directory of the application on which it depends or in a subdirectory of that application.

User Subdirectories

If several different users will be using an application once it is loaded, it is best to create a subdirectory for each user off the application area so that each user's files will be separate. Further, because one user may use two or more applications, it is doubly important that individual subdirectories be created off the application directory and not the root. In this way each user can have a directory bearing his or her name in each application area. For example, if Jon does both word processing and spreadsheet analysis, then the proper directory structure will look like the one shown below:

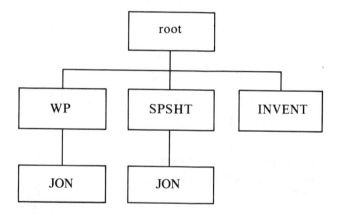

PREPARING THE FIXED DISK FOR SHIPMENT

It is very important that the fixed disk be properly prepared for travel prior to moving it. This requires that the read/write head be retracted to a position that is not over the magnetic medium of the disk. Failure to do this could result in the read/write head contacting the disk, causing damage and loss of data. When the read/write head contacts the disk, it is called a *head crash*.

The exact method of retracting (sometimes called *parking*) the read/write head is determined by the type of computer that you have. However, for IBM PCs, you will find a command called SHIPDISK.COM on the "Guide to Operations" diskette that came with your computer. To prepare your disk for shipment, simply execute that command. For IBM models 30, 50, 60, and 80, you will use the "Reference Diskette" and select the "Move the computer" option. For other types of computers, refer to your owner's manual.

SUMMARY

In this chapter you learned how to manage the fixed disk, including

- How to back up the fixed disk
- How to restore data
- How to use the fixed disk backup routine
- How to use FASTOPEN
- How to load applications onto a fixed disk
- How to prepare your fixed disk for shipment

In the next, and final, chapter of this book, you will learn about managing the entire computer system.

MISCELLANEOUS TOPICS

Congratulations! You have come a long way since Chapter 1. If you have read and worked through the examples in the preceding chapters, you will have no trouble using DOS. This final chapter covers topics and commands that you are unlikely to need. But, just in case, they are presented here. Also presented is a short guide to system maintenance. You may want to skim through this chapter now, so you know what is in it, and come back to it later, should the need arise.

PUTTING DOS ON A FIXED DISK

The fixed disk is usually already formatted and ready for use, so we hope that you will never need the information presented here. However, if your disk fails, you may need to prepare a new one for use. The fixed disk cannot be used before it is prepared and DOS is installed on it. The preparation of the fixed disk is the subject of this section.

WARNING: The commands shown in this section will destroy any existing files on the fixed disk. Do not try these examples unless you are preparing a disk for use for the first time.

Partitioning the Disk

Before the fixed disk can be formatted, it must be partitioned. A *partition* is a portion of the fixed disk that can be either part or all of the disk. You can partition the fixed disk so that it can be used with two or more different operating systems, but we will explain how to prepare the fixed disk for use only with DOS because this is the most likely situation. If your system needs to support another operating system, such as XENIX, you must refer to the specific instructions in your DOS manual.

To partition the fixed disk, use the FDISK external command. Put a copy of the DOS diskette in drive A and start the computer. Once the DOS prompt is displayed, enter the FDISK command. You will see this screen (the version number may vary):

```
IBM Personal Computer
Fixed Disk Setup Program Version 3.30
(C)Copyright IBM Corp. 1983,1987

FDISK Options

Current Fixed Disk Drive: 1

Choose one of the following:

     1.   Create DOS Partition
     2.   Change Active Partition
     3.   Delete DOS Partition
     4.   Display Partition Information
     5.   Select Next Fixed Disk Drive

Enter choice: [1]


Press ESC to return to DOS
```

Most of these options (and others that you will see shortly) are primarily for use by programmers or system integrators who are preparing a disk for a unique application. You will need only the first option. Because 1 is the default selection, simply press ENTER now. You will see this screen:

```
Create DOS Partition

Current Fixed Disk Drive: 1

     1. Create Primary DOS partition
     2. Create Extended DOS partition
```

```
Enter choice: [1]

Press ESC to return to FDISK Options
```

Again, you want the first selection, which is the default, so press ENTER now.

What you see next depends upon the state of the fixed disk. If, by chance, a DOS partition was created by someone else, you will see the following message:

```
Primary DOS partition already exists.
```

If this occurs, just press ESC until you are back at DOS and skip to the section in this chapter called "Installing DOS Using SELECT."

If a partition does not already exist, you will see this screen:

```
Create Primary DOS Partition

Current Fixed Disk Drive: 1

Do you wish to use the maximum size
for a DOS partition and make the DOS
partition active (Y/N).............? [Y]

Press ESC to return to FDISK Options
```

You should answer yes, the default, by pressing ENTER. (You would not want to give DOS the largest partition when two or more operating systems will be using the same disk—a very rare situation.)

The largest partition that can be created and used by DOS is 32 megabytes. Because many fixed disks are larger than this, you can create a second DOS partition that is accessed as a separate drive. (This will be discussed shortly.)

After pressing ENTER, you will see the following message:

```
System will now restart

Insert DOS diskette in drive A:
Press any key when ready . . .
```

Press a key.

If you will not be creating a second DOS partition, skip ahead to the section called "Installing DOS Using SELECT."

Creating a Second DOS Partition

After the system has restarted, execute FDISK and select option 1 from the first options menu. You will again see this screen:

```
Create DOS Partition

Current Fixed Disk Drive: 1

    1. Create Primary DOS partition
    2. Create Extended DOS partition

Enter choice: [1]

Press ESC to return to FDISK Options
```

This time select option 2, and you will see prompts similar to those for creating the first partition. Answer them in the same fashion as before.

Once you have completed the process, DOS will treat the second partition as drive D.

Installing DOS Using SELECT

The easiest way to install DOS on a fixed disk is by using the SELECT command. (If your version of DOS does not include SELECT, skip to the next section.) Recall that SELECT is used to load DOS on a disk. When the command was explained, only floppy disks were discussed, but the process is the same for the fixed disk. In addition to formatting the DOS partition and copying the DOS system files, SELECT is used to specify the country and keyboard layout. The example that follows installs DOS for the United States and England.

Recall that SELECT has the general form

SELECT *target country-code keyboard-code*

where *target* is the drive specifier for the drive that will receive DOS. The values for the *country-code* and *keyboard-code* are found in Chapter 11.

With the DOS disk in drive A, enter the following command:

```
SELECT C: 001 US
```

You will see this warning:

```
SELECT is used to install DOS the first
time.  SELECT erases everything on the
specified target and then installs DOS.
Do you want to continue (Y/N)?
```

Answer yes. You will now see this stronger warning:

```
WARNING,  ALL DATA ON NON-REMOVABLE DISK
DRIVE C: WILL BE LOST!
Proceed with Format (Y/N)?
```

Answer yes again. The formatting process will take several minutes. When the formatting is completed, you will see this message:

```
Format complete
System transferred

Volume label (11 characters, ENTER for none)?
```

Enter the volume label of your choosing. SELECT then copies DOS onto the hard disk.

Now remove the DOS disk from drive A and press CTRL-ALT-DEL simultaneously to restart the computer. If you have done everything correctly, DOS will now load from drive C.

Installing DOS Using FORMAT

If your version of DOS does not have the SELECT command, you must use the FORMAT command.

Put your DOS work disk in drive A and enter the following command:

```
FORMAT C: /V /S
```

The /S causes the DOS system files to be transferred, and /V tells FORMAT to request a volume label. The formatting will take several minutes to complete. When it is done, you will see this message:

```
Format complete
System transferred

Volume label (11 characters, ENTER for none)?
```

Enter the volume label of your choosing.

Recall that the /S option only transfers the DOS hidden system files, not the DOS external commands. To copy these commands to the fixed disk, enter the following command:

```
COPY A:*.* C:
```

Now remove the DOS disk from drive A and press CTRL-ALT-DEL simultaneously to restart the computer. If you have done everything correctly, DOS will now load from drive C.

THE SET COMMAND

The SET command is used to create and give a value to a name that becomes part of DOS's environment. Although this name may not be of any direct value to you, it may be used by application programs. The general form of SET is

SET *name=value*

where *name* is the string that is placed into DOS's environment with the value of *value*.

For example, the following command sets the name APPSDAT to the path \PROGRAM \APPS.

```
SET APPSDAT=\PROGRAM\APPS\
```

Once this is done, an application program that wants to know where application program data files are can check the value of APPSDAT in the DOS environment.

To remove a name from the environment, use the general form

SET *name=*

For example, the following command removes APPSDAT.

```
SET APPSDAT=
```

You can use the value of a name stored in the environment in a batch file by placing the name between percent signs. For example, the following batch file uses the value of APPSDAT to copy data files from the path specified by the value of APPSDAT into the current working directory.

```
REM copy the data files into the current working directory
COPY %APPSDAT%*.*
```

When this batch command runs, it will look like this:

```
COPY \PROGRAM\APPS\*.*
```

RECOVERING FILES FROM A DAMAGED DISK

In rare cases a disk will become damaged in such a way that part of a file will still be readable. In such cases you can partially recover the file by using the RECOVER command. However, this sort of recovery will only be useful on text files where a small amount of text will have to be reentered. If part of a program file is lost, the program will simply not run. The general form of RECOVER is

RECOVER *file-name*

where *file-name* is the name of the file to recover, which may include a drive specifier and a path.

For example, to recover a file named TED on drive C, use the following command.

```
RECOVER C:TED
```

You can use RECOVER to recover an entire disk when it is the disk's directory that has become damaged. When a disk's directory is damaged, it is unreadable, so DOS cannot know which files are on the disk. In this type of recovery operation the program files may be recovered in a usable form, but it is best not to rely on this. To recover an entire disk, use this form of RECOVER:

RECOVER *drive-specifier*

As RECOVER recovers the files, it does not know their names (because the directory is unreadable), so it puts them in files using this form of name: FILEnum.REC, where *num* is a number between 0001 and 9999.

Never assume that you can successfully recover a lost file; often there is no way to do so. It is usually better to simply go to a backup copy. But if an accident does occur, you can try RECOVER.

MAINTAINING YOUR SYSTEM

A computer is much like an automobile. With proper care and attention, it will run for several trouble-free years. But if you neglect the maintenance, it will be plagued with troubles. A computer system requires two types of care: (1) physical maintenance of the computer and (2) maintenance of the software.

Maintaining the Hardware

The golden rule of maintaining the computer's hardware is to keep it clean. Dust is the computer's worst enemy. It can build up on the circuits inside the computer, causing them to overheat by reducing their normal heat-dissipation capabilities. Further, dust and dirt on diskettes reduces the life of both the diskettes and the disk drive read/write heads.

Though it may be hard to believe, static electricity is a major cause of computer failure. Walking across a carpet on a dry winter day can cause your body to develop a charge of several thousand volts. If you touch the wrong part of the computer, this voltage could flow into the circuits and literally blow their insides apart! If static electricity is a problem in your environment, you can either use antistatic sprays on the carpet or invest in a grounded metal strip that you always touch first before touching the computer.

Along the same lines as static electricity is lightning. If lightning strikes very near the computer, enough of the charge can be picked up by the circuits to destroy them. You cannot prevent lightning, but you can minimize the risk by unplugging the computer from power. The wires that carry power act like a large antenna, which can pick up the lightning charge. If your computer is unplugged, there is much less chance of damage.

Finally, don't put liquids on top of the computer. Although this seems like a simple statement, nonusers, unfamiliar with computers, often will put coffee cups or soft drink cans on top of the system. Obviously, a spill can cause significant damage.

Maintaining the Software

The most important thing that you can do to protect the software in the system is to maintain a rigid backup schedule. The average system usually has several years of information stored in it, and the dollar value of this information is often far greater than the cost of the computer. It is a resource to be protected.

In large (or even small) offices it is important to restrict access to any computer that contains important information. Though deliberate destruction of information is rare, it can happen. Most of the time, however, the damage is done by someone literally not knowing what they are doing—the "bull in a china shop" syndrome. Every employee must have a clear understanding that the information in the computer is a valued asset. The fact that it is "invisible" does not reduce its importance.

Application programs are often improved by their developers and you will want to take advantage of these new versions. To avoid trouble, you must switch to the new version correctly. First, never destroy an old version of the program! Sometimes, though rarely, the new version will have an unknown problem that prevents it from being used. If you have destroyed the old version, you will have no way to run the application. Second, always follow the installation instructions that come with the new version. Unless specifically told otherwise, if you run the application from a fixed disk, make sure that all the old programs are replaced by the new ones. Mixing different versions of the programs that make up an application can cause serious trouble.

FINAL THOUGHTS

DOS is somewhat like a living animal because it continues to evolve and change as the ways in which it is used evolve. The knowledge and understanding that you have gained about DOS will benefit you both now and in the future, because the same basic concepts can be applied to other environments. In fact you will probably be using DOS on one computer and a different operating system on another in the not too distant future. You can easily generalize your understanding of DOS, and you will have no trouble using virtually any type of computer or operating system.

QUICK COMMAND REFERENCE

This appendix contains a short summary of all DOS commands, presented in alphabetical order. The purpose of this appendix is to help you quickly learn what a command does or find which command you should use for a certain operation. For a full discussion of each command, please refer to the text.

The following notational conventions will be used. Items enclosed between square brackets ([ ]) are optional. Except where explicitly noted otherwise, the term *path* refers to the full path name, including an optional drive specifier. The term *file name* may include a drive specifier and/or a path name. Finally, three periods (...) indicate a variable-length list, and two periods (..) indicate a range such as 1..10.

For most commands, the complete general form of the command is shown. However, commands that have very rarely used options are shown in their most common form.

APPEND

The external APPEND command is used to join one directory to another. If directory B is joined to A, it will appear to the user that directory A contains all of A's and B's files. APPEND is executed the first time using one of the following two forms:

APPEND *path1*[;*path2*;..*pathN*]

or

APPEND [/X] [/E]

The first form uses APPEND's default method of operation, in which you have access to the appended directory but cannot see the files in a directory list of the directory appended to or execute a command. APPEND is an installed command. The second form is used to install APPEND. The /X option causes all files in the appended directory to show up in a listing of the directory they are appended to. Also, programs in the appended directory can be executed from within the directory appended to. The /E option causes the appended paths to be held in the DOS environment area. APPEND is used to allow access to data files much as PATH is used to allow access to program files.

You can see the currently appended directories by simply entering the APPEND command with no arguments. The following form disassociates any appended directories:

APPEND ;

For example, the following command appends the \WP directory:

```
APPEND \WP
```

ASSIGN

The external ASSIGN command is used to redirect input/output (I/O) operations from one disk drive to another. It takes the general form

ASSIGN *drive1*=*drive2* [*drive3*=*drive4* ...]

For example, to reverse the assignments of drives A and B, you could use the following command:

```
ASSIGN A=B B=A
```

Now all I/O operations for A will go to B, and all I/O operations for B will be redirected to A.

You reset the drives to their original assignments by entering ASSIGN with no arguments. Remember, do not use ASSIGN with the BACKUP or PRINT commands.

ATTRIB

The external ATTRIB command is used to set or examine the archive and read-only file attributes. It takes the general form

ATTRIB [+R] [−R] [+A] [−A] [*file-name*] [/S]

where *file-name* is the name of the file(s) that will have its attributes set or examined. Wildcard characters are allowed. +R turns on the read-only attribute, while −R turns it off. The +A turns on the archive attribute, while −A turns it off. If one of these is not present, the current state of the file attributes is displayed. The /S option tells ATTRIB to process files in the current directory and any subdirectories.

For example, the following command turns on the read-only attribute for all .EXE files in the current directory.

```
ATTRIB +R *.EXE
```

BACKUP

The external BACKUP command is used primarily to back up the contents of a fixed disk by copying it to several floppy diskettes. Used in this way, it takes the general form

BACKUP *source-drive* [*file-name*] *target-drive* [/A] [/D:date]
[/F] [/L] [/M] [/S] [/T:time]

The *file-name* may include wildcard characters.

The meaning of each BACKUP option is shown below:

Option	Meaning
/A	Add files to existing target diskettes
/D:date	Copy only those files with dates the same as or later than *date*
/F	Format the target diskette before copying
/L	Create and maintain a log file
/M	Copy only those files that have been modified since the last backup
/S	Process all subdirectories
/T:time	Copy only those files with times equal to or later than *time* on the specified date

For example, if executed from the root directory of drive C, the following command backs up the entire fixed disk.

```
BACKUP C: A: /S
```

BREAK

The internal BREAK command tells DOS to check more frequently for the CTRL-BREAK key combination, which is used to cancel commands. It takes the general form

BREAK [*ON*]

or

BREAK [*OFF*]

Though setting BREAK to ON may seem tempting, it is usually not a good idea because it slows down the execution of all commands and programs.

The following command tells DOS to check more frequently for the CTRL-BREAK key combination.

```
BREAK ON
```

CALL

The CALL batch command is used to execute another batch file command from within a batch file. The general form of CALL is

CALL *batch-file*

where *batch-file* is the name of the batch file command that you wish to execute.

For example, the following command calls the batch file named COPYALL.BAT.

```
CALL COPYALL
```

CHCP

The internal CHCP command is used with code page switching for extended foreign language and country support. This little-used command is seldom required. Refer to your DOS manual.

CHDIR

The internal CHDIR command (CD) is used to change the current directory. The general form of the command is

CHDIR *path*

where *path* is the path name of the directory you are changing to. For example, the following command makes the \WP directory current.

```
CHDIR \WP
```

CHKDSK

The external CHKDSK command reports the status of the specified drive and repairs certain types of disk errors. It takes the general form

CHKDSK [*drive-specifier*][*file-name*][/F][/V]

If *drive-specifier* is absent, the current disk is checked. The /F option instructs CHKDSK to fix any errors that it can. The /V option displays all files and their paths. Specifying a *file-name,* which may include wildcard characters, causes CHKDSK to report the number of noncontiguous (nonadjacent) sectors used by the file(s).

For example, the following command reports the status of drive A and attempts to fix any errors.

```
CHKDSK A: /F
```

CLS

The internal CLS command clears the screen of the computer's display monitor.

COMP

The COMP external command is used to compare two files. It has the general form

COMP *first-file second-file*

where *first-file* and *second-file* are file names that may contain wildcard characters.

For example, the following command compares the contents of the file ACCOUNTS.DAT on drive A to the file by the same name on drive B.

```
COMP A:ACCOUNTS.DAT B:ACCOUNTS.DAT
```

COPY

The internal COPY command is used to copy the contents of one file into another. It takes the general form

COPY *source destination* [/V]

where *source* is the name of the file to be copied into *destination*. Both file names may use wildcard characters. The /V option causes COPY to automatically verify that the information was copied correctly into the destination file.

For example, the following command copies all files that begin with the extension EXE to the C drive.

```
COPY *.EXE C:
```

CTTY

The internal CTTY command is used to switch console control to a different device, such as a remote terminal. It takes the general form

CTTY *device-name*

where *device-name* must be one of DOS's standard device names. Do not try this command unless there is actually another device attached to your computer that can control it.

DATE

The internal DATE command is used to set the date of the system. It takes the general form

DATE [*date*]

where *date* is the current date. You must use the proper date convention for the country you live in. For the United States, it is mm-dd-yy. If you do not specify *date* on the command line, DATE reports what it thinks is the current date and waits for you to either enter the correct date or press ENTER, indicating that you accept the date reported.

For example, the following command sets the date to June 26, 1988:

```
DATE 6-26-88
```

DEBUG

The external DEBUG command is used by programmers to help find problems in programs. (You may not have DEBUG in your version of DOS.)

DEL

The internal DEL command erases files from a disk. It takes the general form

DEL *file-name*

where *file-name* is the name of the file to be erased. You can use wildcard characters in the file name to erase groups of files. ERASE is another name for DEL.

For example, the following command erases all files that begin with INV from the disk in drive B.

```
DEL B:INV*.*
```

DIR

The internal DIR command is used to list a disk's directory. It has the general form

DIR [*file-name*] [/P] [/W]

If a file name is present, only those files that match the file name will be displayed. Otherwise, the entire directory is listed. Wildcard characters are allowed in the file name. The /P option pauses the display every 23 lines, while the /W option causes the directory to be displayed in four columns across the screen.

For example, the following command lists only those files with the extension BAT.

```
DIR *.BAT
```

DISKCOMP

The external DISKCOMP command is used to compare two diskettes for equality. Its most common form is

DISKCOMP *first-drive second-drive*

where *first-drive* and *second-drive* are drive specifiers.

For example, the following command compares the diskette in drive A with the one in drive B.

```
DISKCOMP A: B:
```

DISKCOPY

The external DISKCOPY command is used to make a copy of a diskette. Its most common form is

DISKCOPY *source destination*

where *source* and *destination* are drive specifiers. DISKCOPY cannot be used to copy the fixed disk.

For example, the following command copies the diskette in drive A to the one in drive B.

```
DISKCOPY A: B:
```

ECHO

The ECHO batch command is used to write messages to the screen and turn on or off the echoing of other batch commands. It takes this general form

ECHO [on] [off] [*message*]

For example, the following command prints the message "Backing up all files" to the screen.

```
ECHO Backing up all files
```

EDLIN

The external EDLIN command is used to create and maintain text files. It has the general form

EDLIN *file-name*

where *file-name* is the file to be edited. EDLIN recognizes the following commands:

Command	Meaning
A	Append lines (from disk file)
C	Copy lines
D	Delete lines
E	End edit and save file
I	Insert lines
L	List lines
M	Move lines
P	Display a page (23 lines)
Q	Quit —does not save file
R	Replace text
S	Search text
T	Transfer lines (merges one file into another)
W	Write lines (to file)
line-num	Edit *line-num* specified

For details, refer to Chapter 7.

ERASE

The internal ERASE command erases files from a disk. It takes the general form

ERASE *file-name*

where *file-name* is the name of the file to be erased. You can use wildcard characters in the file name to erase groups of files. DEL is another name for ERASE.

The following command erases all files that have the extension DAT from the disk in drive B.

```
ERASE B:*.DAT
```

FASTOPEN

The external FASTOPEN command allows DOS to remember the location of files that are in deeply nested subdirectories, thus providing faster access to these files. Its general form is

FASTOPEN *drive-specifier* [=*num*]

where *num* determines the number of files that DOS will remember. This number can be in the range of 10 through 999; the default is 34. FAST-OPEN is an installed command; that is, you can only execute it once each time the computer is turned on.

For example, the following command causes DOS to remember the location of 34 files on the fixed disk.

```
FASTOPEN C:
```

FDISK

The external FDISK command is used to partition the fixed disk when it is first prepared for use. Refer to Chapter 14 for details.

FIND

The external FIND command searches for occurrences of a string in a list of files. FIND is a filter that sends its output to the standard output device, which may be redirected. The general form of FIND is

FIND [/C] [/N] [/V] *"string" file-list*

where *string* is the string searched for and *file-list* is the list of files to search. Notice that the options must precede the string.

The /C option causes FIND to display a count of the occurrences. The /N option causes the relative line number of each match to be displayed. The /V option causes FIND to display those lines that do not contain the string.

For example, the following command searches the files REC1.DAT and REC2.DAT for the string "payroll".

```
FIND "payroll" REC1.DAT REC2.DAT
```

FOR

The FOR batch command is used to repeat a series of commands using different arguments. The FOR command takes the general form

FOR *%%var* IN (*argument list*) DO *command*

where *var* is a single-letter variable that will take on the values of the arguments. The arguments must be separated by spaces. The FOR will repeat *command* as many times as there are arguments. Each time the FOR repeats, *var* will be replaced by an argument moving from left to right.

For example, the following command prints the files TEXT1, TEXT2, and TEXT3.

```
FOR %%F IN (TEXT1 TEXT2 TEXT3) DO PRINT %%F
```

FORMAT

The external FORMAT command is used to prepare a diskette for use. Its most common form is

FORMAT *drive-specifier* [/V]

The diskette to be formatted must be in the specified drive. The / V option causes FORMAT to prompt you for a volume label.

Remember that formatting a disk destroys any and all preexisting data, so use the FORMAT command with care.

For example, the following command formats the disk in drive A.

```
FORMAT A:
```

GOTO

The internal GOTO batch command is used to direct DOS to execute the commands in a batch file in a nonsequential order. Its general form is

GOTO *label*

where *label* is a label that is defined elsewhere in the batch file. When the GOTO is executed, it causes DOS to go to the specified label and begin executing commands from that point. With GOTO, you can cause execution to jump forward or backward in the file.

For example, the following command causes execution to jump to the label DONE.

```
GOTO DONE
```

GRAFTABL

The external GRAFTABL command loads a character table that gives DOS extended foreign language support. It requires a color/graphics adapter. If you speak English, you will not need this command.

GRAPHICS

The external GRAPHICS command enables graphics images to be printed on the printer using the print-screen function. Its general form is

GRAPHICS [*printer*] [/ R] [/ B/] [/ LCD]

where the name of *printer* is determined according to the list below:

Printer Type	Name
IBM Personal Graphics Printer	GRAPHICS
IBM Proprinter	GRAPHICS
IBM PC Convertible printer	THERMAL
IBM Compact printer	COMPACT
IBM Color printer with black ribbon	COLOR1
IBM Color printer with red, green, and blue ribbon	COLOR4
IBM Color printer with cyan, magenta, yellow, and black ribbon	COLOR8

If no printer name is specified, the IBM Personal Graphics Printer is assumed. The Epson MX-70, MX-80, and MX-100 printers are quite commonly used with microcomputers and are also specified with the GRAPHICS printer name.

By default, white on the screen is printed as black on the printer and black on the screen is printed as white. The / R option causes black to print as black and white to print as white. The background color of the screen is usually not printed, but if you have a color printer, you can print the background by specifying the / B option. Finally, the / LCD option should be specifed for computers using the IBM PC Convertible Liquid Crystal Display.

For example, the following command enables graphics images to be printed using the default GRAPHICS printer.

GRAPHICS

IF

The IF batch command takes the general form

IF *condition command*

If the *condition* evaluates to TRUE, the *command* that follows the condition is executed. Otherwise, DOS skips the rest of the line and moves on to next line (if there is one) in the batch file. (Refer to Chapter 8 for details.)

JOIN

The external JOIN command joins one drive to the directory of another. Thus files on the first drive may be accessed from the joined drive as if they were in a subdirectory. JOIN takes the general form

JOIN *joining-drive joined-drive \ directory* [/ D]

The *joining-drive* will appear to be in the specified directory of the *joined-drive*. The / D option is used to disconnect a join.

For example, this joins the A drive to the C drive using the directory ADRIVE.

```
JOIN A: C:\ADRIVE
```

KEYB

The external KEYB command loads keyboard information for foreign language support. Its most common form is

KEYB *keyboard-code,code-page*

where *keyboard-code* and *code-page* are determined using Table A-1. If you speak English, you will not need this command.

For example, the following command configures the keyboard for use in Germany.

```
KEYB GR,437
```

Country	Keyboard Code	Code Page Code
Australia	US	437
Belgium	BE	437
Canada — English	US	437
Canada — French	CF	863
Denmark	DK	865
Finland	SU	437
France	FR	437
Germany	GR	437
Italy	IT	437
Latin America	LA	437
Netherlands	NL	437
Norway	NO	865
Portugal	PO	860
Spain	SP	437
Sweden	SV	437
Switzerland — French	SF	437
Switzerland — German	SG	437
United Kingdom	UK	437
United States	US	437

TABLE A-1   The DOS Keyboard and Code Page Codes

LABEL

The external LABEL command is used to create or change a disk's volume label. It has the general form

LABEL [*drive-specifier*] [*name*]

If no *drive-specifier* is used, then the current disk is assumed. If you do not specify the volume *name* on the command line, you will be prompted for one. Disk volume labels may be up to 11 characters long. You cannot use the following characters in disk volume labels:

* ? / \ ¦ . , ; : + = < > [ ]

For example, the following command changes the volume label on the current disk to MYDISK.

```
LABEL MYDISK
```

LINK

The external LINK command is used only by programmers. (You may not have LINK in your version of DOS.)

MKDIR

The internal MKDIR command (MD for short) is used to create a subdirectory. Its general form is

MKDIR *path*

where *path* specifies the complete path name to the directory. The path name may not exceed 63 characters in length.

For example, the following command creates the directory \WP\FORMS:

```
MD \WP\FORMS
```

MODE

The external MODE command is used to set the way that various devices operate. MODE is a very complex command with several different forms. (Refer to Chapter 11 for details.)

MORE

The external MORE command allows you to page through a text file 23 lines at a time. It is a filter that reads standard input and writes to standard output. Its most common form is

MORE <*file-name*

where *file-name* is the file to be viewed.

You can also use MORE in conjunction with other commands, such as DIR, to provide a convenient way to page through displays that are larger than one screen. For example, the following command displays the directory 23 lines at a time.

```
DIR ¦ MORE
```

NLSFUNC

The external NLSFUNC command is used by versions of DOS greater than or equal to 3.30 to provide extended support for non-English users. You will probably never need to use it. For details, refer to your DOS user's manual.

PATH

The internal PATH command is used to define a search path that DOS uses to locate program files in directories other than the current one. It takes the general form

PATH *path[;path . . .;path]*

where *path* is the specified search path. You define multiple search paths by separating each path with a semicolon. There cannot be spaces in the path list.

For example, the following command defines a path to the \WP \FORMS directory.

```
PATH \WP\FORMS
```

PAUSE

The PAUSE batch command is used to temporarily stop a batch file's execution. It takes the general form

PAUSE [*message*]

If the *message* is present, it will be displayed. PAUSE waits until a key is pressed.

PRINT

The external PRINT command prints text files on the printer. Its most common form is

PRINT *file-name file-name* ... *file-name* [/T] [/C]

where *file-name* is the name of a file you want printed. The /T option cancels the PRINT command. The /C option cancels the printing of the file name it follows.

For example, the following command prints the files LETTER1.WP and LETTER2.WP.

```
PRINT LETTER1.WP LETTER2.WP
```

PROMPT

The internal PROMPT command is used to change the DOS prompt. It takes the general form

PROMPT *prompt*

where *prompt* is the desired prompt. The prompt string can contain one or more special format commands that allow greater flexibility. The commands are shown below:

Command	Meaning
$$	Dollar sign
$b	¦ character
$d	System date
$e	Escape character
$g	> character
$h	A backspace
$l	< character
$n	Current drive letter
$p	Current directory path
$q	= character
$t	System time
$v	DOS version number
$_	Carriage return-linefeed sequence

For example, one of the most popular prompts is created by the following command:

```
PROMPT $p$g
```

It displays the current directory path followed by the > symbol.

RECOVER

The external RECOVER command attempts to recover damaged files. It has the general form

RECOVER [*drive-specifier*] [*file-name*]

If only the drive specifier is present, RECOVER attempts to recover all files on a disk. Otherwise, only the specified file is recovered. When the entire disk is recovered, RECOVER creates file names following this convention: FILEnum.REC, where *num* is a number between 1 and 9999.

Remember, not all files can be recovered. Further, recovered program files are very likely unusable. It is best to use RECOVER only on text files—and then only as a last resort.

For example, the following command attempts to recover the file FORMLET.WP.

```
RECOVER FORMLET.WP
```

REM

The REM batch command has the general form

REM *remark*

The *remark* can be any string from 0 to 123 characters in length. No matter what the remark contains, it will be completely ignored by DOS.

For example, the following remark is ignored.

```
REM this is a sample batch file remark
```

RENAME

The internal command RENAME (REN for short) is used to change the name of a specified file. It takes the general form

RENAME *old-name new-name*

where *old-name* and *new-name* are file names.

For example, the following command changes the name of the file originally called INV.DAT to INV.OLD.

```
RENAME INV.DAT INV.OLD
```

REPLACE

The external REPLACE command replaces files on the destination disk with those by the same name on the source disk. It takes the general form

REPLACE *source destination* [/A] [/P] [/R] [/S] [/W]

If you specify the /S option, all files in all subdirectories will also be examined and replaced. You can use /A to add to a disk only those files that are not currently on the destination disk. This prevents existing files from being overwritten. If you need to insert a different diskette before REPLACE begins, use the /W option. This causes REPLACE to wait until you press a key before beginning. The /P option causes REPLACE to ask you before a file is replaced.

For example, the following command replaces the files on A with those by the same name found on B, including all subdirectories.

```
REPLACE B: A: /S
```

RESTORE

The external RESTORE command is used to restore files to the fixed disk from diskettes created using BACKUP. It takes the general form

RESTORE *backup fixed* [/A:date] [/B:date] [/E:time] [/L:time] [/P] [/S]

where *backup* is a drive specifier defining the drive that holds the backup diskette and *fixed* is a drive and path specifier for the fixed disk. The options are summarized in table below:

Option	Meaning
/A:date	Restore all files modified on or after the specified date
/B:date	Restore all files modified on or before the specified date
/E:time	Restore all files modified at or earlier than the specified time on a given date
/L:time	Restore all files modified at or later than the specified time on a given date
/M	Restore all files that have been modified or deleted since the last backup
/N	Restore only those files that do not exist on the fixed disk
/P	Prompt before restoring a file
/S	Restore all subdirectories

For example, the following command restores all files having the DAT extension into the DATA directory using drive A to read the backup diskettes.

```
RESTORE A: C:\DATA\*.DAT
```

RMDIR

The internal command RMDIR (RD for short) is used to remove a subdirectory. It has the general form

RMDIR *directory*

where *directory* is a complete path name to the desired directory. The specified directory must be empty. It is not possible to remove a directory that still has files in it.

For example, the following command removes the WP directory.

```
RMDIR \WP
```

SELECT

The external SELECT command is used to install DOS on a new disk and allows you to define the country and keyboard codes. Its general form is

SELECT *source target country-code keyboard-code*

where *source* is the drive specifier of the drive that holds the DOS disk and *target* is the drive specifier of the drive that holds the new disk. See Table A-1 for the country codes. The keyboard codes are shown below:

Country	Code
Arabic	785
Australia	061
Belgium	032
Canada — English	001
Canada — French	002
Denmark	045
Finland	358
France	033
Germany	049
Israel — Hebrew	972
Italy	039
Netherlands	031
Norway	047
Portugal	351
South America	003
Spain	034
Sweden	046
Switzerland	041
United Kingdom	044
United States	001

Caution: SELECT must only be used on a new disk because it destroys any preexisting information.

For example, the following command prepares the disk in drive B for use in the United States. The DOS disk is assumed to be in drive A.

```
SELECT A: B: 001 US
```

SET

The internal SET command is used primarily by programmers and system integrators to put a name and its value into DOS's environment. (Refer to Chapter 14 for details.)

SHARE

The external SHARE command is used in networked systems to prepare for file sharing and file locking. Refer to your networking and DOS manuals for complete information.

SHIFT

The SHIFT batch command is used to shift the command line arguments left one position. This allows for more than 10 arguments.

SORT

The external SORT command sorts text files on a line-by-line basis. It is a filter command that reads standard input and writes to standard output. It takes the general form

SORT [<*input*] [>*output*] [/R] [/+*num*]

where *input* and *output* are either file names, devices, or pipes. If not specified, standard input and output are used. The standard default is ascending order (A to Z). The /R option causes the file to be sorted in reverse or descending order. The /+*num* causes the sorting to begin with the *num*th column.

For example, the following command produces a sorted directory listing.

```
DIR ¦ SORT
```

SUBST

The external SUBST command allows you to use a different drive specifier to access a drive and directory. That is, you can use SUBST to assign a drive specifier to a drive and directory and refer to that drive and directory by using the drive specifier. In essence the new drive specifier is like a nickname for the other drive. SUBST takes the general form

SUBST *nickname drive-specifier path*

where *nickname* is the new drive specifier for the indicated drive specifier. The *path* is the path to the desired directory.

To undo a substitution, use this form of the command:

SUBST *nickname* /D

For example, this causes drive A to respond to both A: and E:.

```
SUBST E: A:\
```

SYS

The external SYS command is used to copy the DOS system files to a disk. It has the general form

SYS *drive-specifier*

where *drive-specifier* indicates the drive that will receive the system files. SYS does not transfer COMMAND.COM, however. SYS must be able to read the system files off the current drive.

For example, the following command puts the system files on the disk in drive B.

SYS B:

TIME

The internal TIME command is used to set the system time. It takes the general form

TIME [*hh:mm:ss*]

If you do not enter the time on the command line, you will be prompted for it. TIME expects the numbers 0 through 23 for the hours; that is, it operates like military, 24-hour clocks. You need not specify the seconds.

For example, the following command sets the time to 12 noon.

TIME 12:00:00

TREE

The external TREE command prints a list of all directories on the specified disk. It has the general form

TREE *drive-specifier* [/F]

where *drive-specifier* is the letter of the drive that will be examined. If /F is used, the files in each directory are also displayed.

For example, the following command displays the directory structure for the disk in A.

TREE A:

TYPE

The internal TYPE command displays the contents of a file on the screen. It has the general form

TYPE *file-name*

where *file-name* is the file to be displayed.
For example, the following command displays a file called TEST.

TYPE TEST

VER

The internal VER command displays the DOS version number. It takes no arguments.

VERIFY

The internal VERIFY command turns on or off verification of disk write operations. That is, when turned on, it confirms that the data written to disk is exactly as it should be and that no errors have taken place. It takes the general form

VERIFY [ON]

or

VERIFY [OFF]

where you specify either on or off.

For example, the following command turns verification off.

```
VERIFY OFF
```

VOL

The internal VOL command displays the volume label of the specified disk. It has the general form

VOL [*drive-specifier*]

where *drive-specifier* is the name of the drive whose volume label will be displayed. If not specified, the volume label of the current drive is displayed.

For example, the following command displays the volume label of the current drive.

```
VOL
```

XCOPY

The external XCOPY command is a more powerful and flexible version of the COPY command. It takes the general form

XCOPY *source target* [/A] [/D] [/E] [/P] [/S] [/V] [/W]

where *source* and *target* are file or path names. The operation of XCOPY is largely determined by the options applied to it. These options are summarized in the table below:

Option	Meaning
/A	Copy only those files with the archive attribute turned on; the state of the archive bit is not changed
/D:date	Copy only those files whose date is equal to or later than the one specified
/E	Create all subdirectories, even if empty

Option	Meaning
/M	Copy only those files with the archive attribute turned on; the state of the archive bit is turned off
/P	Prompt before copying each file
/S	Copy files in subdirectories
/V	Verify each write operation
/W	Wait until a disk is inserted

For example, the following command copies all files on a disk in A to one in B, including all subdirectories.

```
XCOPY A: B:\ /S
```

TRADEMARKS

AT™   International Business Machines Corporation
DOS™   International Business Machines Corporation
IBM®   International Business Machines Corporation
PS/2™   International Business Machines Corporation
XT™   International Business Machines Corporation

INDEX

The manuscript for this book was prepared and submitted to Osborne/McGraw-Hill in electronic form.

The acquisitions editor for this project was Jeffrey Pepper. The technical reviewer was Kevin Shafer. Lyn Cordell was the project editor.

Text type is Times Roman. Display type is Univers.

Cover art is by Bay Graphics Design Associates. Cover supplier is Phoenix Color Corporation. This book was printed and bound by R. R. Donnelley & Sons Company, Crawfordsville, Indiana.

Other related Osborne/McGraw-Hill titles include:

1-2-3® Made Easy
by Mary Campbell

Osborne's famous "Made Easy" format, which has helped hundreds of thousands of WordStar® users master word processing, is now available to Lotus® 1-2-3® beginners. *1-2-3® Made Easy* starts with the basics and goes step by step through the process of building a worksheet so you can use Lotus' spreadsheet with skill and confidence. Each chapter provides a complete 1-2-3 lesson followed by practical "hands-on" exercises that help you apply 1-2-3 immediately to the job. When you've got worksheets down, you'll learn to create and print graphs, manipulate 1-2-3's data management features, use advanced file features . . . even design keyboard macros. As the author of *1-2-3®: The Complete Reference*, and a columnist for IBM® PC UPDATE, ABSOLUTE REFERENCE, and CPA JOURNAL, Mary Campbell has plenty of experience with 1-2-3. With her know-how, you'll soon be handling 1-2-3 like a pro.

$18.95 p
0-07-881293-3, 400 pp., 7³⁄₈ x 9¹⁄₄

WordStar® 4.0 Made Easy
by Walter A. Ettlin

WordStar® Made Easy, the original "Made Easy" guide with 350,000 copies sold worldwide, has been so successful that Osborne has published a companion volume on the new WordStar® version 4.0. All 4.0 commands and features are thoroughly described and illustrated in practical exercises so you can put WordStar to immediate use, even if you've never used a computer before. Walter Ettlin, who has written four books and taught high school for 23 years, guides you from the fundamentals of creating a memo or report to using WordStar's calculator mode, macro commands, and Word Finder™. You'll also learn to use WordStar's latest spelling checker. *WordStar® 4.0 Made Easy* puts you in control of your software with the acclaimed "Made Easy" format now found in 11 Osborne titles. (Includes a handy pull-out command card.)

$16.95 p
0-07-881011-6, 300 pp., 7³⁄₈ x 9¹⁄₄

dBASE III PLUS™ Made Easy
by Miriam Liskin

Liskin's *Advanced dBASE III PLUS™* and Jones' *Using dBASE III PLUS™* have been so successful that we're filling in the gap for beginners with *dBASE III PLUS™ Made Easy*. Learning dBASE III PLUS™ couldn't be simpler. You'll install and run the program, enter and edit data. Discover all the features of using dBASE III PLUS at the dot prompt. Each concept is clearly explained and followed by examples and exercises that you can complete at your own speed. Liskin discusses sorting and indexing, performing calculations, and printing reports and labels. Multiple databases are emphasized, and Liskin presents strategies for working with them. You'll also find chapters on customizing the working environment and exchanging data with other software. If you're curious about higher-level use, Liskin's final chapter shows how to combine the commands you've learned into batch programs so you can begin to automate your applications. (Includes two command cards for quick reference.)

$18.95 p
0-07-881294-1, 350 pp., 7³⁄₈ x 9¹⁄₄

DisplayWrite 4™ Made Easy
by Gail Todd

Upgrading from DisplayWrite 3™ to DisplayWrite 4™? Here's the book that provides a thorough introduction to IBM's word processing software. Handle new menus, screens, and options with ease as Todd leads you from basic steps to more sophisticated procedures. The famous "Made Easy" format offers hands-on exercises and plenty of examples so you can quickly learn to produce letters and reports. All of DisplayWrite 4's new features are covered, including printing interfaces; the voice add-on; Paper Clip, the cursor control that lets you take up where you left off; and Notepad, a convenience that enables you to insert notes into documents. Todd, the author of numerous user guides and manuals, has the know-how to get you up and running fast.

$19.95 p
0-07-881270-4, 420 pp., 7³⁄₈ x 9¹⁄₄

WordPerfect® Made Easy
by Mella Mincberg

Here's the book that makes learning WordPerfect®
quick, easy ... even enjoyable. With Mincberg's
follow-along lessons, this IBM® PC compatible word
processing software will be at your command in just a
couple of hours. Edit text, save and print a document,
set tabs, format pages. You'll become a skillful Word-
Perfect user as you work through practical applications. When you're ready to explore more sophisticated WordPerfect features, Mincberg is there with
detailed instructions to help you run WordPerfect's
spell checker and mail merge, manage files, create
macros, and use special enhancements like windows
and line numbering. Mincberg, author of the ever-so-
useful *WordPerfect®: Secrets, Solutions,
Shortcuts*, draws on her years of computer training
experience to help you become an assured, savvy
WordPerfect user. (Includes quick-reference command
card.)

$18.95 p
0-07-881297-6, 400 pp., 7³/₈ x 9¹/₄

Microsoft® Word Made Easy,
Second Edition
by Paul Hoffman

Hoffman's top-selling *Microsoft® Word Made Easy*
has been revised to cover Microsoft's latest version
of this widely used word processing software. Both
beginning and experienced users will find a clear
presentation of Word's new features, "made easy" for
immediate application. Hoffman covers text outlining,
spelling correction, hyphenation, creating indexes and
tables of contents, and laser printers. Word's new
functions, style sheets, windows, and glossaries are
described in depth, and you'll find extra tips for using
the mail-merge function. In the tradition of Osborne's
"Made Easy" series, all techniques are explained with
practical hands-on examples and are illustrated with
helpful screen displays.

$16.95 p
0-07-881248-8, 300 pp., 7³/₈ x 9¹/₄

Your IBM® PC Made Easy
(Includes IBM PC (DOS 2.0) And PC-XT)
by Jonathan Sachs

*"In one word, OUTSTANDING! Perfect for beginning
and advanced users, an excellent tutorial/reference.
A very thorough guide to most facets of your IBM
PC, from PC-DOS, hardware, software, resources
supplies, batch files, etc. Rating: A"
(Computer Book Review)*

$14.95 p
0-07-881112-0, 250 pp., 7¹/₂ x 9¹/₄

C Made Easy
by Herbert Schildt

With Osborne/McGraw-Hill's popular "Made Easy"
format, you can learn C programming in no time. Start
with the fundamentals and work through the text at
your own speed. Schildt begins with general concepts,
then introduces functions, libraries, and disk input/
output, and finally advanced concepts affecting the
C programming environment and UNIX™ operating
system. Each chapter covers commands that you can
learn to use immediately in the hands-on exercises
that follow. If you already know BASIC, you'll find
that Schildt's C equivalents will shorten your learning
time. *C Made Easy* is a step-by-step tutorial for
all beginning C programmers.

$18.95 p
0-07-881178-3, 350 pp., 7³/₈ x 9¹/₄

DOS: The Complete Reference
by Kris Jamsa

Why waste computing time over a baffling PC-DOS™
command or an elusive MS-DOS® function? *DOS:
The Complete Reference* has the answers to all
of your questions on DOS through version 3.X. This
essential resource is for every PC- and MS-DOS user,
whether you need an overview of the disk operating
system or a reference for advanced programming and
disk management techniques. Each chapter begins
with a discussion of specific applications followed by
a list of commands used in each. All commands are
presented in the same clear, concise format: description, syntax, discussion of arguments or options, and
examples. For comprehensive coverage, *DOS: The
Complete Reference* discusses Microsoft® Windows and EDLIN, and provides two special appendixes
covering the ASCII chart and DOS error messages. A
ready resource, *DOS: The Complete Reference*
is the only DOS consultant you'll need.

$27.95 p, Hardcover Edition
0-07-881314-x, 840 pp., 7³/₈ x 9¹/₄

$24.95 p, Paperback Edition
0-07-881259-3, 840 pp., 7³/₈ x 9¹/₄

1-2-3®: The Complete Reference
by Mary Campbell

1-2-3®: The Complete Reference is the authoritative desktop companion for every Lotus® 1-2-3® user. All commands, functions, and procedures are explained in detail and are demonstrated in practical "real-world" business applications. Conventionally organized according to task, this essential reference makes it easy to locate information on topics such as printing, macros, graphics production, and data mangement. Each chapter thoroughly describes a 1-2-3 task and all the procedures it requires, followed by an alphabetical listing of every command or function applied. Special emphasis is placed on compatible software packages, including Report Writer™, Reflex™ and others, that you can use to extend 1-2-3's capabilities. Campbell, a consultant and writer whose magazine columns appear monthly in *IBM PC UPDATE*, *Absolute Reference*, and *CPA Journal*, draws on her years of 1-2-3 expertise to provide you with this outstanding, comprehensive resource.

$25.95 p, Hardcover Edition
0-07-881288-7, 928 pp., 7³/₈ x 9¹/₄

$22.95 p, Paperback Edition
0-07-881005-1, 928 pp., 7³/₈ x 9¹/₄

C: The Complete Reference
by Herbert Schildt

Once again Osborne's master C programmer and author Herb Schildt, shares his insight and expertise with all C programmers in his latest book, *C: The Complete Reference*. Designed for both beginning and advanced C programmers, this is an encyclopedia for C terms, functions, codes, applications, and more. *C: The Complete Reference* is divided into five parts, each covering an important aspect of C. Part one covers review material and discusses key words in C. Part two presents an extensive summary of C libraries by category. Part three concentrates on various algorithms and C applications and includes information on random number generators as well as artificial intelligence and graphics. Part four addresses interfacing efficiency, porting, and debugging. Finally, part five is for serious programmers who are interested in C++, C's latest direction. The book also includes complete information on the proposed ANSI standard

$27.95 p, Hardcover Edition
0-07-881313-1, 740 pp., 7³/₈ x 9¹/₄

$24.95 p, Paperback Edition
0-07-881263-1, 740 pp., 7³/₈ x 9¹/₄

dBASE III PLUS™: The Complete Reference
by Joseph-David Carrabis

This indispensable dBASE III PLUS™ reference will undoubtedly be the most frequently used book in your dBASE III® library. *dBASE III PLUS™: The Complete Reference* is a comprehensive resource to every dBASE III and dBASE III PLUS command, function, and feature. Each chapter covers a specific task so you can quickly pinpoint information on installing the program, designing databases, creating files, manipulating data, and many other subjects. Chapters also contain an alphabetical reference section that describes all the commands and functions you need to know and provides clear examples of each. Carrabis, author of several acclaimed dBASE books, discusses the lastest features of dBASE III PLUS, including networking capabilities; the Assistant, a menu-driven interface; and the Applications Generator, a short-cut feature for creating database files and applications without programming. *dBASE III PLUS™: The Complete Reference* also includes a glossary and handy appendixes that cover error messages, converting from dBASE II to dBASE III PLUS, and add-on utilities.

$25.95 p, Hardcover Edition
0-07-881315-x, 600 pp., 7³/₈ x 9¹/₄

$22.95 p, Paperback Edition
0-07-881012-4, 600 pp., 7³/₈ x 9¹/₄

WordPerfect®: The Complete Reference
by Karen L. Acerson

Osborne's highly successful Complete Reference series has a new addition, *WordPerfect®: The Complete Reference*. Every WordPerfect feature, key, menu, prompt, and error message is explained in simple terms for new users, and with sophisticated technical information supplied for those with experience. Acerson, an early member of WordPerfect Corporation who has been helping WordPerfect users get the most from their software since 1983, discusses the techniques for integrating WordPerfect with Lotus® 1-2-3®, dBASE® III, and other widely used software. Here's another ideal desktop companion to add to your collection.

$27.95 p, Hardcover Edition
0-07-881312-3, 675 pp., 7³/₈ x 9¹/₄
$24.95 p, Paperback Edition
0-07-881266-6, 675 pp., 7³/₈ x 9¹/₄

DOS Command Card

[drive:][path]APPEND
[drive:][path][;[drive:][path]...] or
APPEND ;

Define or display the data file search path.
MS-DOS version 3.2

[drive:][path]ASSIGN [drive1 [=] drive2
[...]]

Route disk I/O request for drive 1 to
drive 2

[drive:][path]ATTRIB [+R¦-R][+A¦−A]
[drive:][path]filename[.ext]

Set the file's read-only and archive-
attribute bits

[drive:][path]BACKUP
[drive:[path][filename[.ext]] d:
[/S][/M][/A][/D:mm-dd-yy]

Back up one or more files to another disk

BREAK [ON¦OFF]

Allow or inhibit DOS CTRL-BREAK checking
when DOS functions finish

CHDIR [drive:][path] or CD [drive:[path]

Change or display the current directory on
the specified drive

[drive:][path]CHKDSK
[drive:][path][filename[.ext]] [/F][/V]

Analyze and (optionally) repair directories,
files, and the FAT

CLS

Clear the screen display

[drive:][path]COMMAND [drive:][path][/P][/C
string][/E:nnnnn]

Invoke a secondary command processor

[drive:][path]COMP
[drive:][path][filename[.ext]]
[drive:][path][filename[.ext]]

Compare the contents of the files
specified

COPY [/A][/B] [drive:][path]filename[.ext]
[/A][/B]
[+[[,,]drive:][path]filename[.ext][/A][/B]...]
[drive:][path][filename[.ext]][/A][/B][/V]

Copy the contents of the source file(s) to
the target file(s)

CTTY device_name

Modify standard input (stdin) to point to
an alternate device

DATE [mm-dd-yy] ¦ [dd-mm-yy] ¦ [yy-mm-dd]

Set or display the current system date

DEL [drive:][path]filename[.ext]

Delete the specified file names from disk

DIR [drive:][path][filename[.ext]][/P][/W]

List the files as specified

[drive:][path]DISKCOMP [drive1: [drive2:]]
[/1][/8]

Compare the contents of the disks in
drive 1 and in drive 2

[drive:][path]DISKCOPY [drive1:
[drive2:]][/1]

Copy the contents of the disk in
drive 1 to the disk in drive 2

ECHO [ON¦OFF¦message]

Allow or suppress the screen display of
DOS command names as the command executes
within a BAT file

ERASE [drive:][path]filename[.ext]

Delete the specified file names from disk

[drive:][path]EXE2BIN
[drive:][path]filename[.ext]
[drive:][path][filename[.ext]]

Convert an EXE file specified by the first
file name to a COM file

[drive:][path]FDISK

Define fixed-disk partitions

[drive:][path]FIND [/V][/C][/N] "string"
[[drive:][path][filename[.ext]]

Display all of the lines that contain the
specified string

FOR %%variable IN (set) DO command	Allow iterative processing of DOS commands
[drive:][path]FORMAT drive:[/S][/1][/V][/B][/4]	Format the disk in the specified drive
GOTO label_name	Allow branching within BAT files
[drive:][path]GRAFTABL	Load software to support the display of extended ASCII characters for the color/graphics adapter
[drive:][path]GRAPHICS [printer_type][/R][/B]	Load software to print graphics
IF [NOT] condition command	Allow conditional batch processing condition is one of the following: ERRORLEVEL number string1==string2 EXIST [drive:][path]filename[.ext]
[drive:][path]JOIN [drive: /D] ¦ [drive: path]	Connect a disk drive to a directory
[drive:][path]KEYBxx	Load software for a foreign keyboard
[drive:][path]LABEL [drive:] [volume_label]	Create or modify an 11-character volume label
MKDIR [drive:][path] or MD [drive:][path]	Create the specified subdirectory
[drive:][path]MODE LPT#[:][n][,[m][,P]] *or* [drive:][path]MODE n *or* [drive:][path]MODE [n],m[,T] *or* [drive:][path]MODE COM#[:]baud[,[parity][,[databits] [,[stopbits][,P]]]] *or* [drive][path]MODE LPT#[:]=COM#	Set the characteristics of the system printer, monitor, or asynchronous communications adapter
[drive:][path]MORE	Display data obtained from standard input to standard output a screen at a time
PATH [[drive:]path[;[drive:]path]...]] *or* PATH ;	Define the optional command search path
[drive:][path]PRINT [/B:buffersize][/C][/D:device_name] [/M:maxticks][/P][/Q:maxentries] [/S:timeslice][T] [/U:busyticks] [[drive:][path]filename[.ext]...]	Install the DOS print queue and print the specified file(s)
PAUSE [remark]	Suspend BAT processing and display a prompt for the user to Strike a key when ready...

DOS Command Card

PROMPT [prompt-string]
Set the system prompt as specified. The following metastrings can be used:

$$ Dollar-sign character
$_ carriage return linefeed
$B ¦ character
$D System date
$E ESCape character
$G > character
$H Delete previous character
$L < character
$N Default-drive letter
$P Current directory
$Q = character
$T System time
$V DOS version number

[drive:][path]RECOVER
[drive:][path]filename[.ext] ¦ [drive:]
Recover the specified file(s) or disk drive

REM [remark]
Display remarks from within a BAT file

REN[AME] [drive:][path]filename[.ext]
filename[.ext]
Rename the file provided as specified

[drive:][path]REPLACE
[drive:][path]filename[.ext]
[drive:][path][/A][/P][/R][/S][/W]
Allow selective replacement/addition of files from the source to the target location

[drive:][path]RESTORE drive:
[drive:][path]filename[.ext][/S][/P]
Restore the specified file(s) from the backup device

RMDIR [drive:]path ¦ RD [drive:]path
Remove the specified subdirectory

[drive:][path]SELECT [[A: ¦ [B:]
drive:[path]] country keyboard
Create a DOS disk with the specified foreign-country support

SET [name=[string]]
Define an item in the command environment

[drive:][path]SHARE
[/F:filespace][/L:numlocks]
Install file-sharing software

SHIFT
Shift the command line parameters %0-%n left one parameter

[drive:][path]SORT [/R][/+ column]
Sort and display data received from standard input

[drive:][path]SUBST [drive: drive:path] ¦
[drive: /D]
Substitute a DOS path name with a disk-drive specifier

[drive:][path]SYS drive:
Copy the system files to the specified disk, making it bootable

TIME [hh:mm[:ss[.nn]]]
Set or display the system time

[drive:][path]TREE [drive:][/F]
Display all of the directory paths on a disk and (optionally) the files that they contain

TYPE [drive:][path]filename[.ext]
Display the contents of the specified file

VER	Display the DOS version number
VERIFY [ON | OFF]	Enable or disable disk-write verification
VOL [drive:]	Display the 11-character volume label of the specified drive
[drive:][path]XCOPY [drive:][path]filename[.ext] [drive:][path][filename[.ext]][/A][/D:mm- dd-yy][/E][/M] [/P][/S][/V][/W] *or* [drive:][path]XCOPY [drive:]path[filename[.ext]] [drive:][path][filename[.ext]][/A][/D:mm- dd-yy][/E][/M] [P][/S][/V][/W] *or* [drive:][path]XCOPY drive:[path][filename[.ext]] [drive:][path][filename[.ext]][/A][/D:mm- dd-yy][/E][/M] [/P][/S][/V][/W]	Provide selective copies of the specified file(s) to the target destination. DOS version 3.2

CONFIG.SYS Entries

```
BREAK=[ON|OFF] default OFF
BUFFERS=n default 2 for PC 3 for AT
COUNTRY=nnn
DEVICE=[drive:][path]filename[.ext]
FCBS=n,n default 4,1
FILES=n default 8
LASTDRIVE=letter default E
SHELL=[drive:][path]filename[.ext]
```

Reprinted with permission from *DOS: The Complete Reference* by Kris Jamsa (Osborne **McGraw-Hill**, 1987).